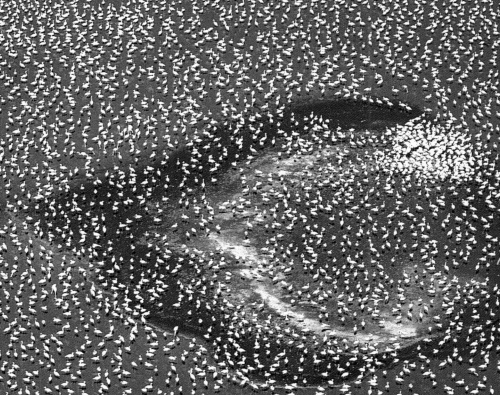

pink africa

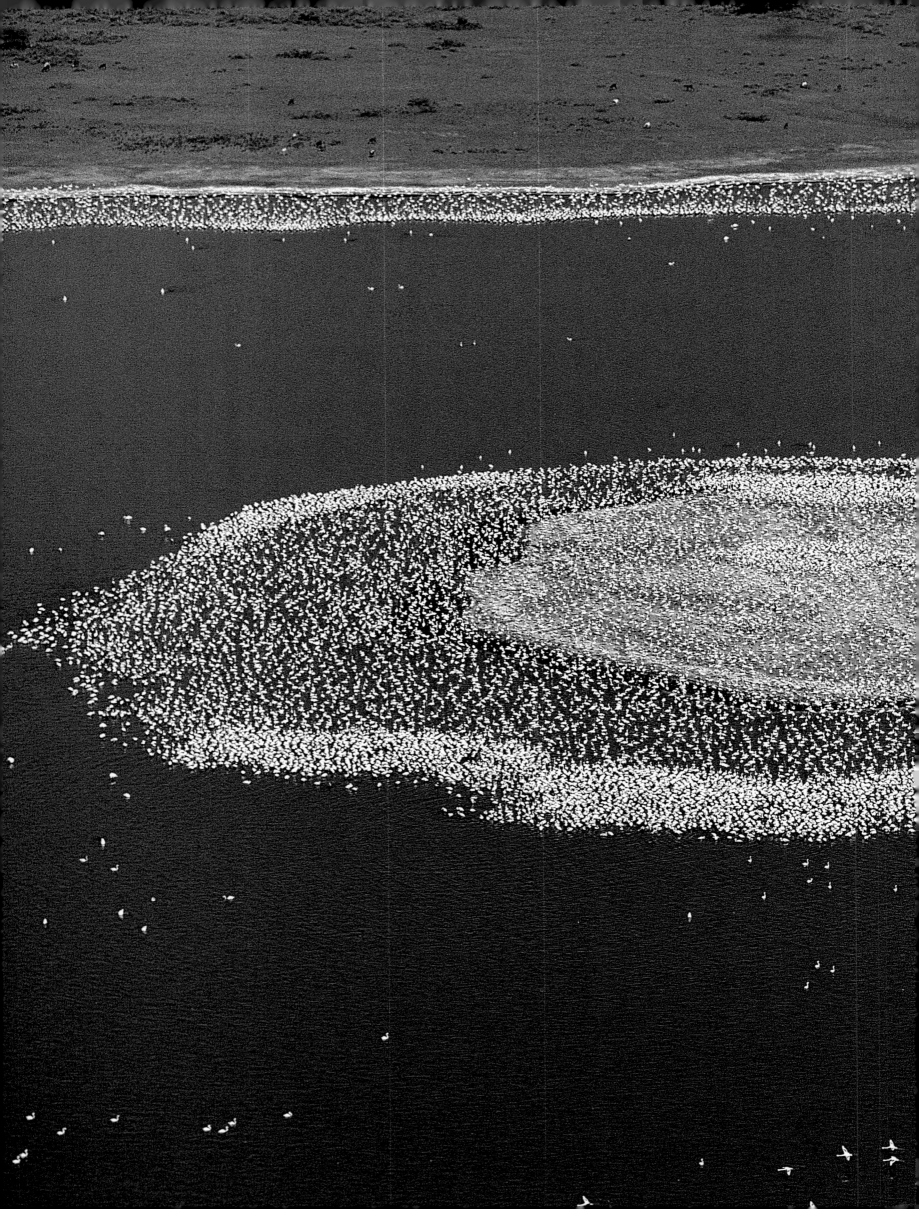

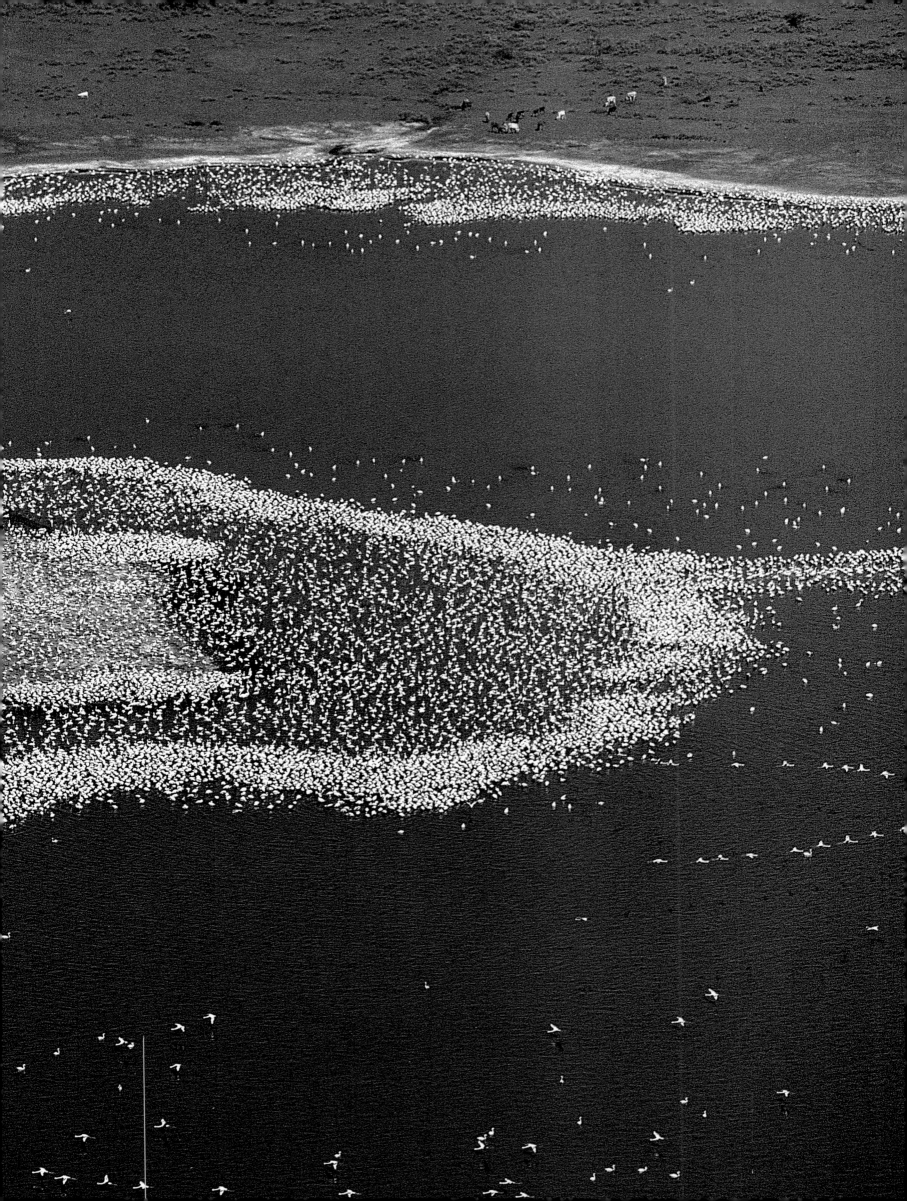

pink africa

PHOTOGRAPHS BY CARLO MARI | TEXT BY NIGEL COLLAR

THE HARVILL PRESS | LONDON

First published in 2000 by
THE HARVILL PRESS
2 Aztec Row
Berners Road
London N1 0PW

www.harvill.com

First Impression

Photographs © Carlo Mari, 2000
Text © The Harvill Press, 2000

The authors have asserted their
moral right to be identified as the
authors of this work

A CIP catalogue record for this
title is available from the British
Library

ISBN 1 86046 804 7

Designed by Olivier Assouline

Originated in Italy by
Sele Offset, Turin
Printed and bound in Italy by
Mariogros-Torino

OPPOSITE:
*The remote Embagai Crater in
Tanzania*
PREVIOUS PAGES:
View of Lake Bogoria in Kenya

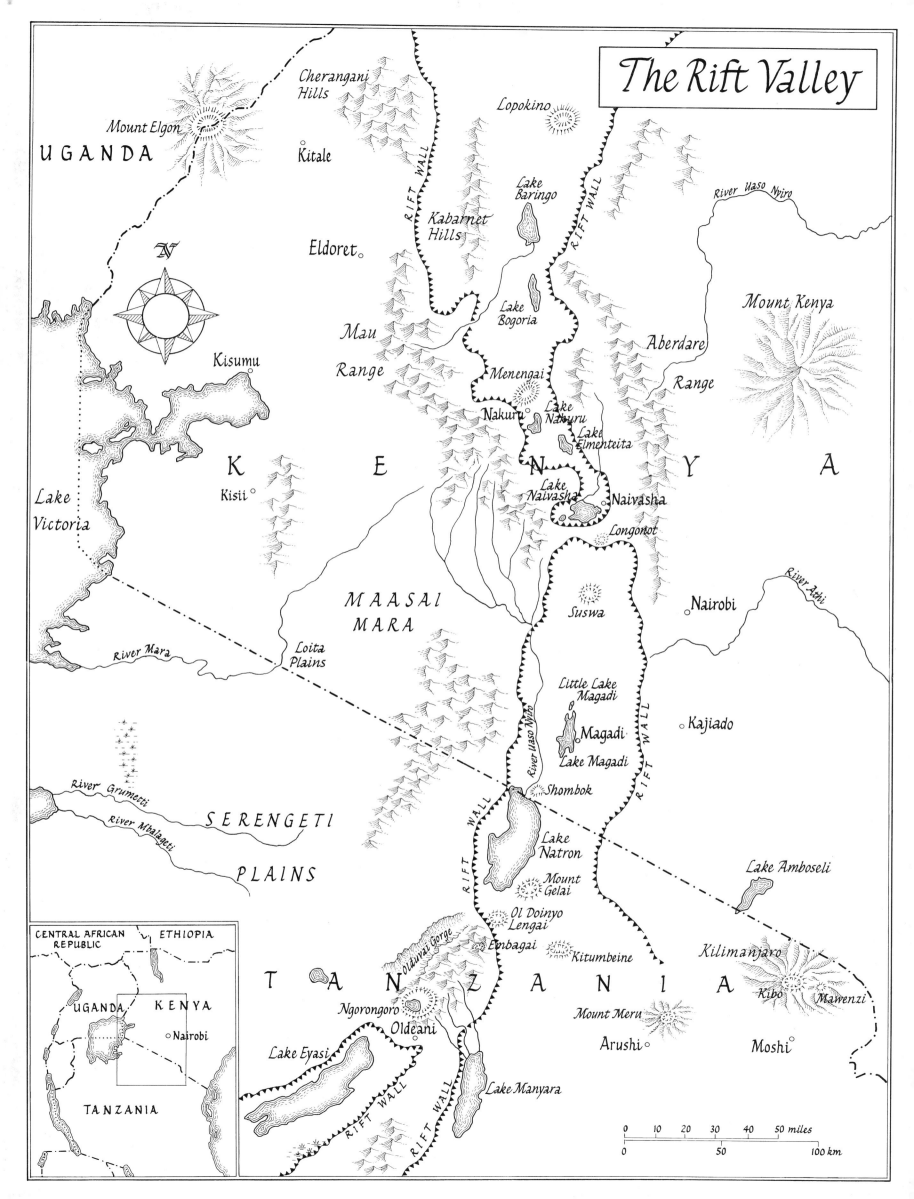

The Rift Valley

UGANDA

Mount Elgon

Cherangani Hills

Kitale

Lopokino

River Uaso Nyiro

Eldoret

Kabarnet Hills

Lake Baringo

RIFT WALL

RIFT WALL

Lake Bogoria

Mau Range

Menengai

Mount Kenya

Aberdare Range

Nakuru

Lake Nakuru

Lake Elmenteita

Kisumu

K   E   N   Y   A

Kisii

Lake Victoria

Lake Naivasha

Naivasha

Longonot

Suswa

Nairobi

River Athi

MAASAI MARA

Loita Plains

River Mara

Little Lake Magadi

Magadi

Kajiado

Lake Magadi

River Uaso Nyiro

RIFT WALL

RIFT WALL

River Grumeti

River Mbalageti

SERENGETI

PLAINS

Shombok

Lake Natron

Mount Gelai

Lake Amboseli

Ol Doinyo Lengai

Olduvai Gorge

Embagai

Kitumbeine

Kilimanjaro

T   A   N   Z   A   N   I   A

Ngorongoro

Oldeani

Mount Meru

Kibo

Mawenzi

Lake Eyasi

Arushi

Moshi

RIFT WALL

RIFT WALL

Lake Manyara

CENTRAL AFRICAN REPUBLIC

ETHIOPIA

UGANDA

KENYA

Nairobi

TANZANIA

| 0 | 10 | 20 | 30 | 40 | 50 miles |

| 0 | | 50 | | | 100 km |

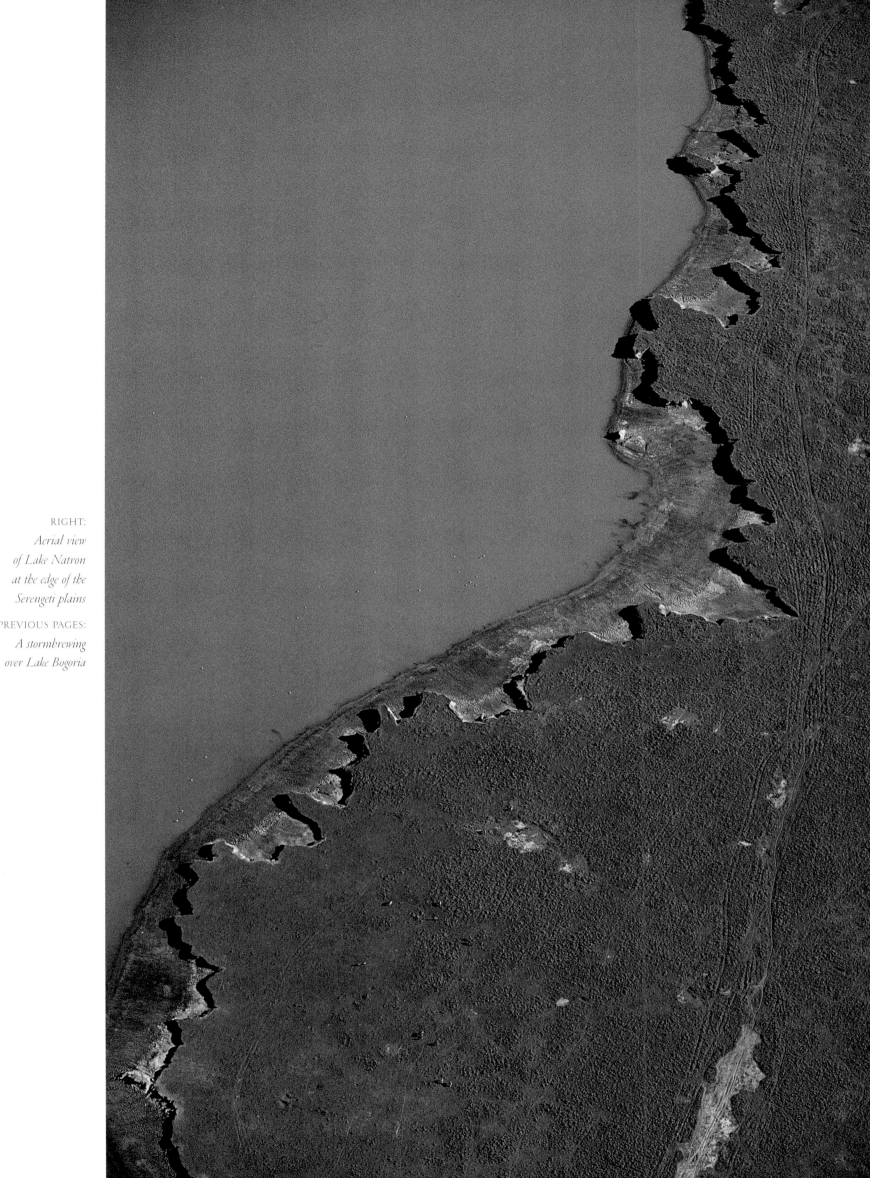

RIGHT:
*Aerial view
of Lake Natron
at the edge of the
Serengeti plains*

PREVIOUS PAGES:
*A storm brewing
over Lake Bogoria*

THE *PHOENICOPTERUS*, OR BURNING WING

— flamingo, flamenco, or flaming one — stands 1.80 m. (6 ft) tall in its pink pallor, coping patiently with a longer neck and legs — relative to its tapering and almost weightless body (a mere 3.6 kg (8 lb) at most) — than any other bird. Its neck curves gracefully up, then over, and ends in an unforgettably ugly, half-hooked schnozzle. When it lowers its head to hide this shameful appendage in murky waters to feed, it holds its crown downwards and points its head back, so that over the ages the upper mandible has atrophied into an upside-down lower mandible, while the lower mandible has outgrown its partner in a new lease of inverse life. With special filters along the inside edges of its bill, it hoovers up tiny animals and organisms in its favoured habitats — muddy warm freshwater lagoons, shallow remote seashores, algae-rich soda lakes. So the flamingo lives life at the margins of things, in places where few other creatures would ever even attempt to survive.

THERE ARE SIX SPECIES:

the Greater Flamingo, *Phoenicopterus roseus*, of Europe, Africa, the Middle East, Central Asia and north-east India, and its very close sister the Caribbean Flamingo, *Phoenicopterus ruber,* of the southern and eastern Caribbean Sea; the Red-kneed Flamingo, *Phoenicopterus chilensis*, of southern South America; the Andean Flamingo, *Phoenicoparrus andinus*, and Puna Flamingo, *Phoenicoparrus jamesi*, of the high Andes; and the millions-strong Lesser Flamingo, *Phoeniconaias minor*, of the Central African Rift Valley and southern African pans. The Greater and Caribbean Flamingos are the biggest species, followed by the Red-kneed and Andean, with the Puna and Lesser being the smallest. Each has a distinctive bill pattern, with different amounts and shapes of colour. The first three are generalists, and can survive in fresh- and saltwater habitats on small mollusks, crustaceans, worms and larvae; the second three are specialists, and feed on the single-cell plants that "bloom" in acrid soda water. Where the generalists have shallow-keeled upper mandibles and small areas of filtering hairs on their bills, the specialists have deep-keeled upper mandibles to increase their complement of filtering hairs, so as to catch sufficient quantities of their tiny prey.

DIFFERENCES BETWEEN THE BILLS OF GREATER AND LESSER FLAMINGOS

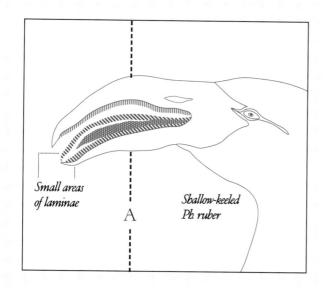
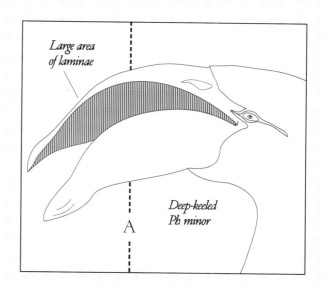

Small areas
of laminae

Shallow-keeled
Ph. ruber

A

Large area
of laminae

Deep-keeled
Ph. minor

A

DIAGRAMMATIC SECTIONS AT ------- A -------

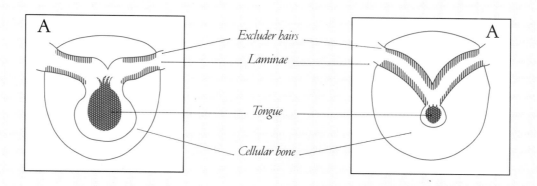

Excluder hairs

Laminae

Tongue

Cellular bone

THEY BUILD A RAISED TURRET OF MUD

and lay usually a single white egg in the shallow bowl atop it. Four weeks of
sitting by both parents produces a grey downy chick which they feed on a bright
red crop-milk. Ten weeks later the chick can take wing as an independent being.
But nesting is usually very sporadic. The birds can hold off for years if conditions
are unpropitious. Consequently numbers increase very slowly. On the other hand
the pollution, disruption and disturbance of their habitats is a worrying modern
trend: the soda-lake species, even the multitudinous Lesser Flamingo, have never
been so precariously balanced as they are today. Fifty million years in the making,
the flamingos will need all our help to make it through just one more millennium.

"No words

I know

can convey

the spectacle

of colour

and motion,

the sound of

their voices,

or the remote

feeling of being

a primitive man

making a discovery

in some archaic

period of time.

To ornithologists

all I can say is

– go and see it

for yourself."

LESLIE BROWN,
The Mystery of the Flamingos

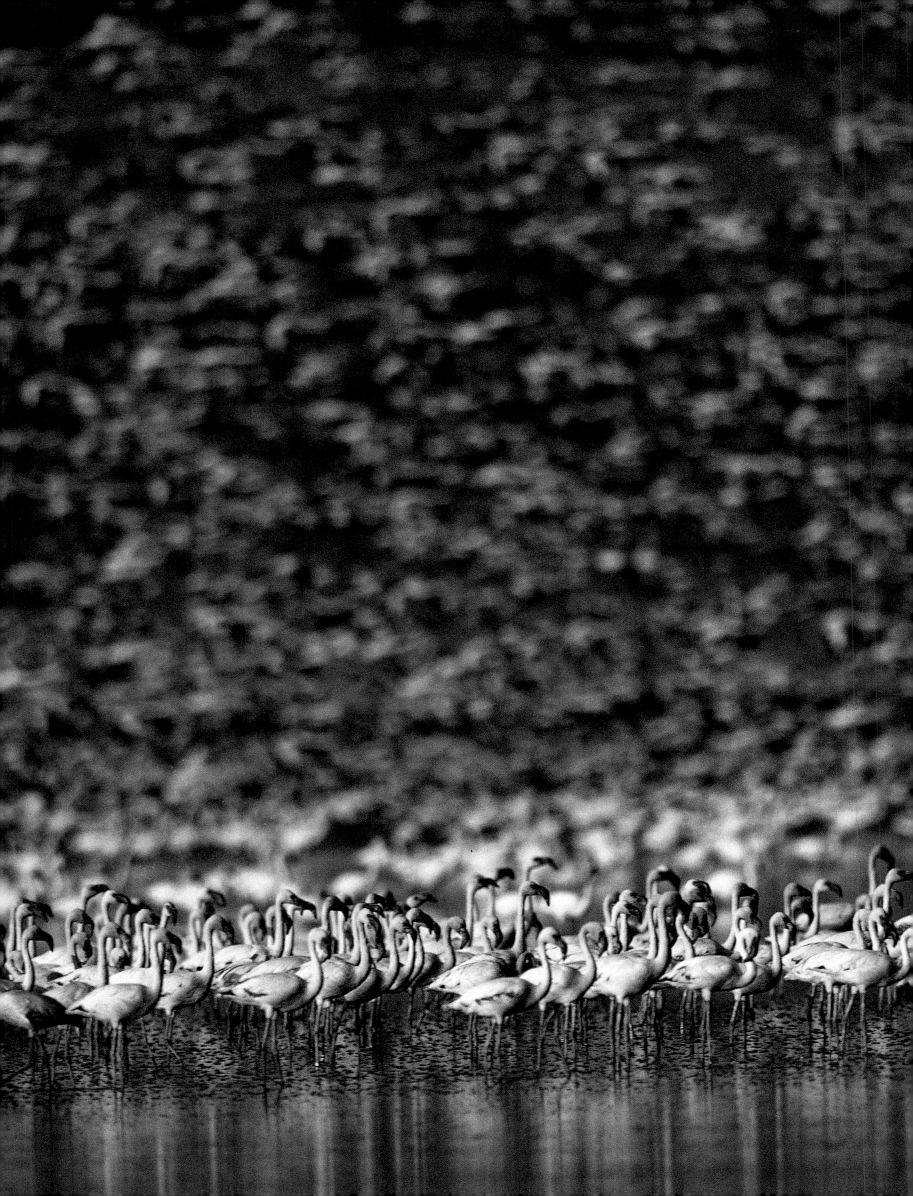

ARRIVE

at the shore of one of six or seven Rift Valley lakes and the pink is just a distant line in the heat haze, a flickering vivid frontier between the burnished blue sky and water. Make your way round to a much closer vantage point and witness the inconceivable, as the line turns into a swathe, a swarm, an immense sweep of birds – ridiculous, unimaginable and exquisite birds. Suddenly they take wing and a wall of pink fire throws itself upwards, obliterating perspective and stopping your heart. Africa turns pink as a hundred thousand, two hundred thousand flamingos, blaze into the sky like a sunset.

Of six million or so flamingos on earth, approximately three-quarters of them live in the soda lakes of the Great Rift Valley. How did it get there, this pinkness at the heart of Africa? How does it contrive simply to *be*? Pink is such an unnatural colour – think pink and at once you conjure synthetic fibres, lipsticks, young girls' dresses and bedrooms – so why is it that this most astonishing of African spectacles overrules our preconceptions and becomes the expression of such glorious life where life itself can barely find another foothold?

The story is ancient, one that begins longer ago than anyone has yet computed. But where did they come from, these irrepressibly graceful yet irredeemably gawky animals? What could possibly count as even a distant relative of such utter eccentrics? Some have thought flamingos are closest to storks – their pelvic structures are similar, and the protein of their eggs resembles that of the stork-related herons. Others have argued for a shorebird ancestry, and, in particular, a link with the delicate, distinctive stilts and avocets: one anomalous wader, the Australian Banded Stilt *Cladorhynchus leucocephalus*, has strong anatomical and behavioural affinities. Yet others feel they are the long-lost cousins of waterfowl – ducks, geese and swans – and certainly to the untrained eye a flamingo bears a vague likeness to a monstrously stretched goose. Its feet are webbed, its feathers waterproof, it can swim and upend, it honks, filter-feeds and flies in flocks, it makes its nest with similar "drawing-in" movements of the head, and its downy chick looks very much like a gosling. There is one further reason for thinking that flamingos are related to waterfowl: the lice that inhabit their feathers – all birds have them – belong to the same genera as those that live on ducks.

Fossil flamingos as many as 50 million years old have been found. This indicates that they evolved very early on in the development of modern birds. They are an extremely ancient group, and their persistence today suggests that they long ago found and filled an ecological niche that no other bird or indeed animal has been able to find or fill. Like the African Rift Valley in which the two most numerous species live, the niche is extremely narrow, but it is very deep and very definite, offering a permanent (insomuch as anything is permanent) home to any creature that can tolerate its conditions and exploit its resources. This is the high risk/high reward syndrome in evolution – if it pays off at all, it does so handsomely. Unsurprisingly, then, you hardly ever see just one or two flamingos: they are not birds to spread themselves around, customarily living in a handful of key sites and nowhere else. But when you do find them, you find them in hundreds, thousands, millions.

This is also the reason that there are very few species of flamingo: the niche they occupy is *so* narrow that, despite the aeons of their existence, there has been precious little scope for diversification. Taxonomists cannot quite agree upon the number of species, but it is either four, five or six. The uncertainty revolves around whether the less specialised forms constitute one, two or three species.

GREATER

Flamingos, *Phoenicopterus roseus* – even when separated out from their American counterpart(s) – are the most familiar and widest spread of them all. Here is the archetypal bird known to all, the one that Lewis Carroll chose to serve as mallets for the croquet game in *Alice in Wonderland*. In fact, it is the least pink of all the flamingos, possessing a whitish head and body with often only a slight tinge of pink. It has a stronger red in the wing-coverts, pink legs, a black-tipped pink bill and, as in all the species, black flight feathers. This gangling animal, which can reach higher than a tall man when stretching in display, ranges all round Africa and the Mediterranean, extending north-east through Turkey and Iran to Kazakhstan, and south-east through the Red Sea and the Persian Gulf to India and Sri Lanka.

Across the Atlantic, in the western and southern Caribbean, lives an extremely similar bird which many consider to be the same species: the Caribbean Flamingo, *Phoenicopterus ruber*, distinguishable from its Old World counterpart by its stronger orange-crimson head, neck and body, and distinctive broad white panel at the base of the bill as far as the eye. This bird breeds at a few sites in the Bahamas, Cuba, Hispaniola, the Netherlands Antilles and Trinidad, plus mainland Mexico and northern Venezuela, and has a most interesting outlying population in Galápagos which, as usual with the animals of Darwin's celebrated islands, shows some remarkably distinct behavioural characteristics.

In southern South America, ranging from sea-level to the high Andean lakes, and from central Peru south to Tierra del Fuego and east to southernmost Brazil, a smaller form is found, the Red-kneed or Chilean Flamingo *Phoenicopterus chilensis*. It possesses the same unspecialised feeding facility as the two larger birds, and thus was once thought conspecific with them, but in reality it is a perfectly distinct species, immediately recognisable by its yellowish legs, red knees and feet, with much more black on the bill than in the two earlier species.

These three forms are the closest to what systematists think were the original flamingos far back in the Eocene, close to the time when the first whales, with some of which flamingos share one key feature, were also emerging. On this basis one might speculate that the ancestor of all modern flamingos arose in the Sea of Tethys (today's Mediterranean) or in the Gulf of Mexico, but in any case rapidly colonising both areas (at a time when the distance between them was far smaller), somewhere in the ten million years following the great K-T event that put an end to the dinosaurs. However, the creation of soda and salt lakes in the African Rift and high Andes – both of which were formed in the past 20 million years – offered a very particular food resource, the grand reward once more beckoning from the dark doorway of chance, which duly led to the evolution of three further species of flamingo, able to outcompete their less specialised ancestors whilst, as a consequence, being tied to more restricted environmental conditions.

The lanky Greater Flaminhgo (right) with its lipstick-pink bill and legs; and the Lesser Flamingo (far right) with its deep-red bill and bright red legs

LESSER

Flamingos, *Phoeniconaias minor,* are — judged on their range — only marginally less successful than the Greater, and rather more so than either the Caribbean or the Red-kneed. Judged on its numbers, however, the Lesser is much the most successful flamingo of them all. Its heartland is the African Rift Valley, with outlying populations in West Africa, southern Africa, and the north-west Indian subcontinent. It is the smallest representative of its family, with a very distinctive dark red bill, generally pink-suffused plumage with crimson streaking on the breast and back, and bold crimson legs. A pity, then, to be called "Lesser" simply on account of its size; so many wonderful birds bear this unfair epithet — Lesser Florican, Lesser White-front, Lesser Grey Shrike, Lesser Whitethroat, Lesser Adjutant — but none is quite so undervalued by the word as the glorious "Lesser" Flamingo.

In the high Andes from Peru south to Argentina two small flamingos were able to evolve as specialist feeders like the Lesser. The Andean Flamingo, *Phoenicoparrus andinus,* is the larger of the two, with a distinctive half-black, half-yellow bill, yellow legs and obvious black flight feathers which form a triangle at the back of the body when standing. The Puna or James's Flamingo, *Phoenicoparrus jamesi,* has a mostly yellow bill, crimson face-patch and legs, and, like the Lesser, which it also rivals in size, crimson streaking on its whiter breast and upperparts.

The fact that this small assemblage of seemingly very similar birds is divided up into three genera is a token of their specialisation. The taxonomists who decided to bestow these genera cleverly retained the prefix *Phoenico-,* meaning crimson, which helps remind us of their essential similarities. All the flamingos share the unmistakable characters of the family — the remarkable coloration, the gabbling and honking calls, the long neck and legs (longer in relation to body size than in any other kind of bird), the elegant tapered body and the unique drooping black-tipped bill wedged into the small head like a squat boomerang. The bill, indeed, is the key to life for the flamingos, a beautifully developed tool that allows them to exploit the narrow but bountiful ecological niche that nature scatters so

haphazardly across the planet. Nevertheless, the differences between the genera are certainly worthy of recognition, for they clearly represent major adaptations of a type which reflect deep ecological differences, even when birds are standing next to one another in the same patch of water.

Both Greater (right) and Lesser (far right) Flamingos hoover up minute organisms in their highly adapted bills

The differences lie in the precise structure of the bill. It is in this feature that the analogy with whales emerges. Look at the picture of a baleen or whalebone whale – preferable a right, genus *Balaena* – and you see an animal with a giant mouth forming a great upward-arching curve from eye to snout, and, when open, a banked wall of baleen plates instead of teeth. Look at the picture of a flamingo and you see something strikingly similar: the line of the upper and lower mandibles, starting just before and below the eye, forms an upward-arching curve that approaches and then runs parallel to the ridge of the upper mandible to its tip.

Both groups of animals have acquired the same fundamental physical attributes for exploiting the great blooms of microscopic creatures that water produces under certain conditions. Just as the whale has evolved plates as extensions of its palate to filter plankton into its body, so the flamingos have developed rows of corneous hair-covered lamellae, equivalent to the whales' baleen plates, along the edges of the mandibles. To ingest foods of appropriate size, but at maximum rates, both the flamingo and the whale need to expose as much as possible of their baleen or hairs, but in such a way as to exclude items too large for processing; the characteristic curve in their mouths helps increase the area across which food gets trapped while keeping out unwanted items which are likely to create blockages and decrease the efficiency of the system.

In the flamingo the tongue works up and down many times a second like a piston (as few as five in Greater, as many as 20 in Lesser): as it retracts, it draws in water and this flattens the hairs, but as it returns it pumps the water out of the mouth, simultaneously causing the hairs to become erect and to catch the waterborne food particles. When enough have been caught, the mandibles are worked together to free the trapped mass of food onto the tongue, which catches it on its rough backward-pointing nodes and draws it down into the oesophagus as it pulses back and forth.

In the less specialised flamingos, the upper mandible, when pictured in cross-section from the front (*see page 17*), is a rather flat oval and the gap between the mandibles is a simple direct opening, an arrangement which allows for a large tongue while minimising the number of lamellae (which are in any case moderately sparsely distributed). In the Lesser Flamingo, by contrast, the upper mandible has a deep keel, so that, when viewed in frontal cross-section, it appears as a downward-pointing triangle. This greatly increases the area over which the lamellae can sit, although it also requires that the tongue becomes much smaller. Held open and looked at sideways on, the bird's bill thus shows a remarkable resemblance to a baleen whale's mouth. The outer lamellae are spaced in such a way as to keep any large particles out, while the inner lamellae are so close together that they serve to trap particles smaller than anything that the unspecialised flamingos would take in. The same thing occurs with the Andean and Puna Flamingos, which differ from one another in the fineness of their filtering lamellae, the smaller Puna Flamingo taking the smallest foods of all, but maintaining an equally large feeding surface along the side of the bill by increasing the depth of the bill and the steepness of the curve of the gape (over 90˚).

It is natural to assume that the Lesser Flamingo is more closely related to the Andean and Puna Flamingos, and that they all developed from a common specialised ancestor at a time when the continents were much closer together. However, it is no less possible that the two groups evolved in parallel from the unspecialised flamingos in the Old and New Worlds respectively, so that, by contrast, they represent the most distant relatives in the family. A token of the distinctiveness of the two Andean specialists is that, unlike all the others, they have lost their hind toes, although this is not necessarily of great taxonomic significance. However, the fact that the Red-kneed Flamingo, whose range embraces theirs, shares the basic bill pattern of the larger species, the Andean Flamingo, tends to suggest that the latter is derived from the former, and not from the red-billed Lesser Flamingo.

ORGANIC

detritus, unicellular algae, larvae of tiny insects, crustaceans, mollusks and sometimes small seeds: all flamingos eat small to minute foods. They obtain this food by walking in water often only a few inches deep, head down and bill submerged, pointing backwards parallel with the water surface. Sometimes they wade into much deeper water; the thighs of flamingos are unfeathered right to the top, indicating their common use of water as deep as the entire length of the leg. However, the food they seek is almost entirely in or on the mud at the bottom of the water: whatever the depth a bird wades to, its neck must be equally long to reach to its feet, so the legs and the neck of flamingos have grown at the same evolutionary speed. Even so, the birds can get deeper still by swimming and upending, which gives them a reach of another foot or more. The webbed feet of flamingos are clearly of use here, but it seems likely that the chief value of the webbing is to prevent such relatively heavy birds from sinking in the soft substrates on which they forage.

In the less specialised flamingos food can vary with locality and season. These birds commonly forage with their heads and necks well submerged, bringing them up every 15 seconds or so in order to breathe. Highly salt-tolerant branchipod crustaceans called brine-shrimps make up most of the diet of European Greater Flamingos, while in East Africa, copepod crustaceans and the larvae of non-biting midges are the main prey. The Caribbean Flamingo mostly consumes small turretshell snails and the larvae of brine-flies. However, both species catch many other small animals, including waterbeetles and crabs, along with the seeds of marsh grasses, sometimes decaying leaves, and of course algae. This is also true of the Red-kneed Flamingo, which forages in a purposeful walk, commonly stirring up small animals as it goes and thus, in winter, attracting swimming Wilson's Phalaropes, *Phalaropus tricolor*, in their wake. All of the less specialised flamingos make use of deliberate foot movements to stir bottom-dwelling larvae and other organisms into the already broth-like suspension through which they sluice their bills.

The more specialised species have evolved to hoover up algae and diatoms in relatively shallow water. The Lesser Flamingo generally feeds in the surface strata of lakes, for which it requires calm conditions, its bill only partly submerged as it filters in blue-green algae such as *Spirulina* and benthic diatoms such as *Navicula*. The bulbous lower mandible holds air, thus helping to serve as a float and allowing the bird to move its head about at a constant depth just beneath the surface. The Andean primarily targets diatoms of the genus *Surirella*, walking rather slowly with fitful pauses, but unlike the Lesser it forages in the bottom few inches of water, not the top, so it frequently upends. The Puna also targets diatoms in haphazard walks in shallow water; whereas the Andean filters out those around 0.8 mm (0.03 in.) long, the Puna takes ones less than 0.6 mm (0.02 in.), enabling the two to live side-by-side in their algae-rich lakes.

Feeding commonly proceeds in small groups, the pattern of dispersal depending on species, and is often done at night. In the Greater Flamingo this nocturnal habit has been thought to be a response to the circadian distribution of brine-shrimps in the water column, but it may also be an adaptation to elevated diurnal predation or disturbance pressures (including the effect of wind on the water surface), or perhaps even simply to help achieve greater thermoregulatory balance. On calm days, Lesser Flamingos will swim far into a lake's centre, feeding as they go, their buoyant heads bobbing up and down over the light waves. But when the wind rises, groups of birds form tight rafts to maintain an area of relatively calm water in which to continue feeding.

Astonishing calculations have been made based on the size of prey, of bird and of feeding flocks. A Caribbean Flamingo, for example, requires something in the order of 270 grammes (9 oz) of food per day, the equivalent of 50,000 brine-fly larvae, so that a flock of 1,500 flamingos would consume 75 million larvae per day, which represents some 27 *billion* larvae per year. Partly because of its smaller size and partly because of its food's greater nutritional value (eating the algae in effect cuts out the middleman), a Lesser Flamingo needs far less than its tall Caribbean cousin – a mere 60 grammes (2 oz) of algae per day. But when one considers that there are more than a million birds present in a region, this represents in reality a daily consumption of 60 tons and an annual consumption of well over 20,000 tons of algae. Such is the concentration of prey species that each Lesser Flamingo merely has to filter 20 litres (5.3 gal) per day to obtain its needs. However, large numbers of birds quickly deplete an area of water, necessitating a change in foraging area as the law of diminishing returns begins to register with them. All the same the birds will generally find sufficient food: one researcher at Lake Nakuru found the water so dense with minute animals that when he put his ear to the surface he could hear their movements, sounding "like the fizzing of a gigantic glass of champagne".

The pigment in the pink and flaming red feathers derives directly from various

carotenes – most importantly canthaxanthin – which are found both in freshwater and saltwater algae. Algae are the richest source of carotenoids. These are broken down by enzymes in the birds' livers to become feather pigments and vitamin A. The reason that the unspecialised flamingos are as pink as the specialised ones lies in the fact that many of the animals they feed on have themselves absorbed the carotene of the algae, passing it directly up the chain to the flamingos.

Flamingos are not, of course, the only pink birds. Their greatest rivals in the claims for pinkness are the savagely flamboyant Scarlet Ibis, *Eudocimus ruber*, and the more restrained Roseate Spoonbill, *Platalea ajaja*, of the mangroves of South America, both of which also feed on items in the food-chain which build on carotenoid-rich algae. Other birds have touches of pink, the most memorable being the almost certainly extinct Pink-headed Duck, *Rhodonessa caryophyllacea*, of the Gangetic floodplain, closely followed by the desperately rare Pink Pigeon, *Columba mayeri*, of Mauritius and the summer-plumaged Rosy or Ross's Gull *Rhodostethia rosea* of the high Arctic. More commonly observed, there is the unforgettable breast of the male European Bullfinch *Pyrrhula pyrrhula*. But none of these birds ever turned an entire lake or sky pink; that privilege is reserved to the flamingos.

In reality, the pink of flamingos is, for the most part, a composite of shades of white and red in the feathers. The flame is in the pale crimson of their wings, most apparent when in flight, and, in the smaller species, in the streaks on their backs and necks. Perhaps the most striking pink in any flamingo is the pale lipstick on the bill and legs of the Greater Flamingo in the Old World. The scientific name, *Phoenicopterus roseus*, means the "rosy crimson-wing"; the closely related Caribbean Flamingo, *Phoenicopterus ruber*, is the "red crimson-wing". The Lesser Flamingo, *Phoeniconaias minor*, is the enchanting "smaller crimson water-nymph". But however much the taxonomists may have sat with their specimens and found expression for their wonder in the word crimson, at any distance the whites and reds of a flock of birds merges into a stunning, shocking pink, as pink as anything that ever coloured a face gracing the cover of *Vogue*.

FLAMINGOS

are birds of wide, shallow or shallow-edged lakes and lagoons in arid, often
sparsely vegetated plains and valleys. Their single most important prerequisite is
to have sufficient food, sufficiently accessible. It appears to be as elementary as
that — always accepting, flamingos being such highly sociable animals, that the
quantities they require are *very* large. At any rate, small water bodies, however
rich the resources they happen to possess, remain essentially unattractive to
them. This aversion can be explained simply in terms of sheer numbers — a small
lake's food supply would be depleted too quickly to sustain a large flock longer
than a few weeks — but this begs the question why so many birds always keep
together as they do. The answer is almost certainly linked to predation: the birds
evidently derive great individual security from remaining in huge compact
flocks. Moreover, it may well be that the water quality of their large lakes also
benefits the birds in this regard, by inhibiting fringing vegetation so that they
have unimpeded views of the surrounding horizon.

The key feature of the habitat of more specialised flamingos is that the water
bears unusually high chemical loads, resulting in the near-monocultural
proliferation of particular resistant organisms. Such water bodies are commonly
volcanic in origin, fed by hot springs, but they also result from run-off into
basins, from which there is no outlet except by evaporation, such that the
mineral content of the water has, over aeons, become highly concentrated. This
does not make them pleasant environments: swimming in Lake Bogoria to
retrieve a shot duck, Leslie Brown, the great hero of flamingo studies in East
Africa, described the water as "viscous and slimy and unbelievably foul".

For Lake Natron he reserved a particular invective. Its dreadful heat "such as
to make one wish one had never been born", appalling smells, treacherous
surfaces and sheer, daunting size combined to draw forth the best of his
boisterous vituperation: evil, fetid, foul, frightful, ghastly, horrible, horrid,
leprous, stinking, vile — all words he used to convey his feelings for the place
both before and after his great discovery there of the Lesser Flamingo's main

breeding grounds in 1954. The less specialised species are commonly found in the same sites, in those parts – or in adjacent areas – where conditions are less harsh and allow a greater variety of foods, but they also inhabit much more usual fresh- and saltwater sites, which nonetheless remain typefied by extensive shallows and sparse fringing vegetation.

The real exception is the offshoot population of Caribbean Flamingos in the Galápagos Islands, which occupy small mangrove-fringed lagoons adjacent to the sea, living and breeding in groups as small as three pairs. But this further substantiates the point about predation: in an environment such as this, where native mammalian predators are absent and native avian ones too small to be worrisome, the flamingo – which spends hours with its head under water – has no need for safety in huge flocks and long views of the shoreline.

Other environmental parameters of importance include the presence of fresh water and the absence of fish. While Greater Flamingos, which use less caustic waters, seem to derive sufficient moisture from their food, Lesser Flamingos, particularly in the stronger chemical lakes, are obliged to drink and bathe in fresh water. They are often seen flying to known temporary or permanent sources, such as rainwater run-off sites, stream outlets, springs and even geysers, to take a few sips and then return to the feeding fray. At Lake Bogoria huge flocks can be seen in the clouds of steam at dawn, waiting their turn to drink. Under stress they will even climb out of the lake onto its rocky shores to drink extremely hot geyser water. Too much fresh water, of course, opens the risk of colonisation by fish, which is bad news for the flamingos – fish being food competitors that can greatly deplete planktonic stocks otherwise exclusively available to the birds. In the Andes, at least, the more favoured lakes are those which either dry out periodically or are too saline for fish to colonise; of course, many of these have no outflow, which represents much the best block on the spread of waterborne food competitors that a flamingo could wish for.

Whether the sites are close to the sea and at sea-level, or far inland and high in the mountains – the Andean species reach some 4,500 m (15,000 ft) – is of no importance. It does not even matter to the birds if the water possesses caustic properties from soda, sulphates, chlorides and fluorides, nor that its temperature in places near springs and geysers approaches 70°C (158°F) – they may, however, dance from foot to foot, waggling their webbed feet in the air, in mild discomfort in the hotter patches of water. What is of real consequence is that food is in abundance – and when only a few organisms can tolerate the more extreme conditions, they develop unimpeded by predation or competition to produce great rafts of rich matter. Flamingos seem entirely indifferent and unflinching in the face of such environmental austerity which permits no other living things to survive. The delicacy and grace of the birds appears all the more extraordinary at the realisation that they are wading in and feeding from water that would instantly burn human skin with its salts and sodas and, in places, simply by its temperature. (Leslie Brown nearly paid very dearly for his discovery of the Lesser Flamingo's breeding grounds: on his first attempt to reach a colony in Lake Natron the soda entered his boots, cutting and burning his feet so badly that he came close to needing a double amputation. He was disabled for six weeks and underwent numerous skin grafts.)

None of this entirely explains the capriciousness which flamingos, and Lesser Flamingos in particular, show over their use of sites. Why in some years they make long risky flights to distant feeding grounds is not known. Why 1,200,000 pairs of Lesser Flamingo decamped for Lake Magadi in 1962, to breed there for the first time that century, remains a total mystery. Why the species fluctuates so dramatically in numbers at Lake Bogoria, when the algal food supply is constant, is no less baffling. Leslie Brown noted that Lake Bogoria is mostly too deep for birds to feed in except by swimming, and that the effects of the daily wind there may make conditions marginally less attractive than the best conditions elsewhere. If, however, the best conditions elsewhere only arise patchily in time and space, Bogoria may often be the birds' first choice – so one can more easily understand why it experiences such an ebb and flow. Even so, Brown also found situations he could not explain – birds deserting lakes just as conditions looked most favourable for breeding, birds arriving at lakes just as the concentrations of salt appeared too

OVERLEAF:
*Dawn finds
Lake Bogoria's
flamingos queuing
to drink in
the steaming
spring water*

low for optimum feeding. Small wonder that he should call his book *The Mystery of the Flamingos*, even after finding their main nesting grounds. Almost certainly the answers lie in the complex interplay of factors at and between every known site, such as long- and short-term rainfall and edaphic patterns, algal productivity cycles, carrying capacities, disturbance and predation levels, distances between lakes, and foraging ease. All this in turn will be influenced by the presence and number of birds already at each site.

There are, certainly, costs to the flamingo in choosing to occupy such extreme environments. Salt sticks to feathers with a vengeance, and needs to be cleaned off regularly: so whereas waterfowl rarely spend more than 10% of their time in feather maintenance, flamingos sometimes have to preen themselves for as much as 30% of theirs. Lesser Flamingos seek out the freshest water in the area, generally where streams run into the lake. The bathing is energetic, the birds submerging their whole bodies, heads and necks, and flapping their wings vigorously as ducks do. Indeed, all their comfort behaviour is much as in other waterbirds, but the spectacle of a flamingo head-scratching is somewhat more amusing than in any other species. When body maintenance is concluded, the birds rest, typically standing on one leg. When they sleep, they face into the wind and either fold the neck into an S and rest the head above the chest, or arrange the neck along the back and rest the head on the rump. At night, when not feeding, they roost on sandbanks or islands, or else in shallow water some distance from the shore.

Flamingos are sociable throughout the year, and perform communal displays whose function appears to create synchrony in breeding activity. This, like the sociability itself, almost certainly relates to predation: the greater the simultaneity of nesting, the greater the chance each nest has of surviving predator attack. The window through which predators have the chance to profit is minimised, so the number of nests they can predate is minimised as well. At any rate, the communal displays may begin many months in advance of a nesting attempt, and sometimes with no such attempt taking place. It seems that, however stable the environment of a flamingo lake may be overall, there are constant fluctuations of productivity within it. Therefore, with each upward movement in a fluctuation, the birds are compelled to prepare themselves in case, this time, the improvement continues to the point where conditions are optimal for breeding.

Pre-breeding displays in Greater Flamingos begin with males gathering in groups, standing erect with the body raised at an angle, neck stretched up and head held at 45°. They then begin "flagging" (shaking) their heads from side to side, calling continuously, which commonly has the effect of drawing females into the group. Individual birds then perform a series of displays, usually beginning with a wing-salute in which the bird stretches as tall as possible, bill vertical, and flicks its wings open and shut. Then it does a twist-preen, snaking its head onto its back, seeming to preen above and below a half-open wing, followed by a wing-flash bow, bending forward, lowering its head to the horizontal, and flicking the wings open and forward to show off the bright crimson upperwing-coverts. It reverts to a twist-preen, and may then pack together with other birds and stand with neck held forward and head arched downwards in a pose known as "hooking".

Lesser Flamingos have more spectacular and more intensely communal displays. A group of birds comes together, their neck feathers partly lifted and a tuft of red raised on each side of the tail, and this in turn stimulates many others to join in. Within a very short time thousands may have packed together. Some raise their heads upwards and flag them from side to side, while others indulge in bill-fencing or adopt broken-neck postures in which the head and bill are dropped onto the breast with a sharp kink in the neck. The mass of birds marches about swiftly together, first one way and then, abruptly, the other, performing these different displays. They push their way blindly through the main flock, their legs a twinkling red forest, drawing in more birds behind them. The congregated raft that results has the appearance of a great protean beast, surging forward with myriad heads and legs, yet with the body steadily floating along as a single entity. On the fringes of such masses, individual birds perform wing-salutes, twist-preens and wing-flash bows.

These communal displays, which may continue daily over many weeks, even months, tend to occur at established sites, two of which are on Lake Nakuru, even though no breeding has been recorded there in over 50 years. Given that sexual maturity in flamingos is delayed until the sixth or seventh year, it is likely that such displays are predominantly the affair of immatures. Throughout these performances, and throughout the individual repertoires, the birds sustain a constant calling. These vary from loud calls accompanied by head-flagging, for example, to sudden low grunts when the wing-salute is given. Indeed, these birds are consistently vocal even when not displaying: keeping up a quiet perpetual burble as they feed, and a strong brassy honking, reminiscent of geese, as they fly. The six species can be told apart on pitch and timbre, but their repertoires are essentially the same.

Among the reasons for such constant hubbub must be the need for members of both new and established pairs to be able to identify one another. The displays may register and stimulate breeding conditions, but they do not promote individual recognition. Voice, on the other hand, is personal, and serves an

Even when mating, the Greater Flamingo continues to combine awkwardness and elegance
Photograph © Hellio & Van Ingen, NHPA

essential function. Pair-bonds certainly carry over from one breeding effort to the next (although, as in many bird species, it may be that breeding failure results in a change of partners), and the birds need to observe strict monogamy in order to ensure that the chances of breeding success are maximised.

BREEDING

success is all the more important in species which only lay a single egg and which do not necessarily breed every year. To perpetuate themselves, the members of a flamingo pair must, like any pair-bonded couple, produce two offspring which survive to sexual maturity. This seems like a relatively modest challenge, but the inherent vulnerability of the birds – their feeding adaptations having rendered them physically defenceless against attacks on their young – means that their best chances of success lie, as previously noted, in the synchronisation of breeding within an entire community. This is especially vital in the less seasonal African lakes. While there might always be enough food for a small number of pairs to breed at virtually any time, their nests would almost inevitably all be predated. Breeding must therefore be postponed until it becomes apparent that the entire lake ecosystem can bear the burden of a large number of birds breeding in one burst.

To date no clear link has been established in East Africa's Lesser Flamingos between food supply, climatic conditions and breeding effort; whilst birds mainly nest in the cool dry season and short rains, there is no guarantee. In southern Africa they only undertake to breed in years when high rainfall has caused extensive flooding. Moreover, in any one breeding attempt only a certain proportion of the adult population participates; in East Africa it may be as little as one-fifth. This is still a considerable number of birds, but when combined with natural gaps in breeding attempts by any of the birds, it suggests how serious the constraints are on a mated pair's ability to produce two surviving offspring.

Pairs intent on breeding will detach themselves from the main pack of displaying birds and perform their own rituals. Sometimes they chase one another, and on rare occasions a male will appear to feed a female. When they mate, the male stalks close behind the female in the hooked-neck posture, mounting her from behind with his feet poised on her wing-joints, opening and fluttering his wings for balance. She leans forward, wings part-open, but will sometimes have the insouciance to carry on feeding, head submerged in the water (as an anthropogenic joke, but also intuitively — she can trust him and can therefore lower her vigilance — one might assume that such "indifferent" females have been paired to the same male for a number years and have seen it all before). Not to be upstaged, he then dismounts over her head.

Mating and indeed initial nest-building activities can occur at lakes other than those on which the birds subsequently breed. Overnight the birds may change their grounds and begin their efforts in earnest elsewhere. Lesser Flamingos generally clump their nests in dense colonies — usually two but sometimes as many as five in a single square metre (11 square feet) —, but on Lake Natron they build along junctions in the soda plates, where mud is soft, so that the resulting pattern is one of short irregular lines of nests. There is a curious tension between nesting pairs in a flamingo colony. They pack together for their greater individual security and appear genuinely disadvantaged if they do not, but they then spend ages bickering with their neighbours, necks writhing and bills open. Sometimes all the birds assert themselves in a territorial display in which they erect the elongated back feathers, often bending their heads towards the nest mound. The result is a delightful sight: watching Lesser Flamingos, Leslie Brown thought of "huge pink feather dusters" whilst, watching the Greater, Sálim Ali conjured the image of "gigantic chrysanthemums".

The nest itself is made of mud. Both members of the pair contribute to the structure, but it is the male who seems most often to initiate the work. At a given site, a bird sits or stands and, using its bill as a dredger and fully stretching its neck, draws mud from the substrate inwards towards itself, compacting it, if sitting, by rocking from side to side and, if standing, by working the feet

Where the soda crust of Lake Natron splits, the softer underlying mud can be used by the Lesser Flamingos for nesting

methodically in a circle. Such excavation creates a little moat around the base of the structure. Lesser Flamingos sometimes suck up bill-fulls of mud and squirt them onto the nest, although this is apparently less frequent than simply scraping with the bill. Even after the egg is laid the work of heightening the nest continues, sometimes frenetically, as an insurance against flooding: the birds doubtless recognise new fresh water in their feeding grounds as a sign of impending rise in lake levels. Usually the final structure is a round, raised concavity (to prevent the egg from rolling off) like a miniature cinder-cone, as much as a foot high and broad enough to take the length of the bird's sitting body; in some conditions it ends up as a short but impressive pillar.

Choice of nesting area is, of course, crucial to the enhanced security of the birds. Lesser Flamingos select sites at considerable distances from the shore,

Territorialism in a colonial bird: the ruffled back feathers tell neighbours to keep their distance from the precious nest

often on semi-exposed islands, making sure that they place a good expanse of hot or caustic mud and water between themselves and any conventional land predators. At Lake Natron they nest *so* far out in the untraversable distance that young birds were believed by the Maasai living around the lake to spring half-grown from the lake's centre: no-one had ever seen an egg to verify that the species did what other birds do. Most flamingos seek out the protection of the remotest, impenetrably soft-surfaced sites, although the less specialised ones will sometimes use stony or sandy islands. Occasionally birds come into breeding condition in advance of having made themselves a nest, and drop their eggs to go to waste on the dry surface of the flats near a feeding area.

The egg is chalky-white and fairly large, as one would expect in the knowledge that the bird inside has to be ready to walk within a week of hatching. If it is lost in the first few days of incubation, a replacement is generally laid; after that the breeding attempt is abandoned. One in 50 nests have two eggs, although some of these appear to result from a female laying in the wrong nest. Incubation begins right away and is undertaken, like nest-building, by both partners working in shifts, their legs bent double underneath them and protruding far out behind. Shifts can be protracted – up to 24 hours in Lesser Flamingos and as many as four days in Greater – although such very long periods almost invariably indicate a problem and the nest fails. Surprisingly, the non-incubating birds can travel great distances in search of good feeding grounds without compromising their reproductive efforts: some Caribbean Flamingos nesting on Bonaire fly 70 km (40 mi) to the Venezuelan coast to forage, and Greater Flamingos from the colony at Fuente de Piedras in southern Spain move 150 km (90 mi) west to feed up in the Coto Doñana. When they return, whether at night or by day, the change-over is rapid and unceremonious. And finally, after 27–28 days of patient sitting in the smaller species, and up to 31 in the larger, the egg begins to hatch. For many hours before the chick emerges it is in vocal contact with the sitting parent, cheeping constantly as it steadily cracks the egg apart. The parent responds, and a crucial bond is established based on voice. Thus, when the chick is creched with thousands of others of similar age and appearance, it is instantly able to distinguish its parents' voices as they return with food. Furthermore, it is the persistent calling of the chick that stimulates the adult to feed it – and indeed to produce the food in question. In captivity such calling has been observed to stimulate food production by a non-breeding adult and even by a seven-week-old youngster.

The newly hatched Lesser Flamingo is covered in grey down and possesses a stubby, straight bill; almost its first act is to eat a fair amount of its own eggshell, doubtless to use the calcium in bone growth. It has soft, swollen, blood-rich legs which cannot initially support its weight. After two days it struggles briefly to its feet. If it falls off the nest cone, the adult must help it back up, without which it is likely to succumb to the temperature of the surrounding mud. The legs shrink, harden and become blackish after five days or so, and by ten days the chick can run with agility. On the nest it is brooded like a duckling between the wing and body of the adult, and it is fed in a manner only otherwise found in pigeons: the adults secrete a bright red crop-milk, the consistency of a watery juice. Rich in protein, lipid fats and glucose, the crop-milk provides the baby flamingo with a powerful and complete growth-promoting diet from the outset. The adult reaches down to the chick — often as it pokes its head from under a wing — and allows the liquid to funnel from its almost closed bill, the nail on the tip of the mandible acting as a precise channel, into the open beak of the youngster whose throat pulses like a man's as it swallows. The feeds are short but numerous

in the early stages, becoming more protracted and less frequent over time. Before two weeks are up the chick is herded into a creche of many hundreds or thousands of birds, and, at around this time, develops a thicker, woollier, brownish-grey down. Eventually as creches themselves unite they may total as many as 300,000 youngsters, guarded by a handful of adults which lead them away from sources of danger (no one understands how these adults select themselves for this duty). However, there is a major risk at this stage, which no adult can do anything to help, which represents another cost of inhabiting such a harsh environment. When drought strikes after the eggs have been laid, water levels drop and even higher concentrations of salts occur. As a result, anklets of soda accumulate around the legs of the chicks, impeding their walking and causing them to fall, soil themselves and slowly perish. At Kenya's Lake Magadi, in 1962, over 100,000 Lesser Flamingo chicks were affected in this way, and although on that occasion a rescue operation was mounted, in the long history of the Lesser Flamingo billions of young must have suffered this miserable fate. Mobility is certainly important to the birds: at Lake Natron and the Etosha Pan the chicks may undertake major treks in great strung-out gaggles – themselves sometimes 30 m (100 ft) long – across the flats in order to reach permanent lagoons, the parents flying in to feed them on the journey while a few adults stay with them throughout. The security of the defenceless young birds is enhanced by the remoteness of their breeding grounds and the areas to which they trek; and at this time many of the adults also go into moult and, for a brief period, become flightless like their offspring, herding themselves together in the most out-of-the-way places. For both adults and young it is imperative to recover or achieve the power of flight as soon as possible. In the chick, the first feathers appear after four weeks, the complete replacement of down is achieved after another three, and at ten weeks it can fly.

By this time the young bird has also acquired the characteristic angled-down bill of the adult, indicating that it is now capable of self-feeding. But despite this relatively short period of dependency, the new recruit will not enter the breeding pool for many years. After a period in dull brown juvenile plumage with black legs and bill, it moults into a succession of immature plumages, very pale with greyish neck and head, before assuming adult-like finery in its third or fourth year. Such delayed maturation is typical of birds of very stable environments, stability implying the long-term availability of food and so the birds are generally found to be at or near the carrying capacity of their environment. When that happens, there is little necessity for producing large numbers of offspring, since they are unlikely to outcompete their fellow birds for food. Instead the emphasis falls on producing a few high-quality offspring who *will* be able to compete successfully for resources. This strategy requires long life in the parents, and long immaturity in the offspring. So it is that a young flamingo may first attempt to breed only when it is three or four years old, although such early attempts invariably fail. In Greater Flamingos the highest breeding success is achieved by seven-year-olds, and they commonly live 20 to 30 years although some have been recorded to reach beyond 50.

For all their efforts to find security in remoteness, untraversable terrain and sheer numbers, flamingos often suffer extensive predation at their breeding colonies. Lesser Flamingos have to deal with African Fish-eagles, *Haliaeetus vocifer*; at one or two lakes from which fish are absent these birds appear to have retrained themselves to specialise on flamingos instead. There are also Egyptian Vultures, *Neophron percnopterus*, which in Africa are renowned for their use of stones to break open the massive eggs of the Ostrich, *Struthio camelus*. Flamingo eggs (and young) present them with far fewer problems. Other vultures and eagles, plus the Marabou, *Leptoptilos crumeniferus*, otherwise known as the Undertaker Bird, also take their toll. Occasionally, even mammals such as hyenas, jackals, cheetahs and servals hunt them down, although because of the sheer numbers of flamingos the overall effect of these predators is negligible. However, Marabous — although for the most part these scavengers are rarely short of a corpse or two when the big flocks are around — have been known to wreak havoc on Greater Flamingos by disturbing nesting colonies simply by walking through them, so that the entire endeavour is abandoned. This happened in the 1960s at Lake Elmenteita to such an extent that measures to control these storks were seriously contemplated.

Of course, the long-suffering flamingos are adapted to cope with such catastrophes, all other things being equal. One way they appear to do this is through their unpredictable use of nesting sites. Although they do not migrate in the normal sense of making major seasonal back-and-forth shifts, they show much more complex opportunist dispersive and exploratory responses which are best explained as reactions to local conditions. To the list of factors already enumerated in explaining their unpredictable patterns of site usage, local accumulations of predators and certain human influences which compromise the birds' security should be added. Whereas migratory birds have an instinctive basis for the direction and distance

First the Greater Flamingo
makes its turret-like nests; then
it feeds its one offspring with
a special crop-milk, as pigeons do

Photograph by M & C Denis-Huot,
© Planet Earth Pictures (above); Photograph
© Helio & Van Ingen, NHPA (opposite)

of their flights, and have, for the most part, a reasonably broad target to aim at in both directions, flamingos are so much more erratic in their displacements, and the targets of their wanderings are so few in number and so restricted in size, that it is hard to believe their brains can be equipped with instinctual maps to guide them. Perhaps it is the case that in flocks of such long-lived birds there are always some individuals of sufficient age to lead them to the alternative sites, and that by this means the knowledge is handed on from generation to generation. It is now suspected that a tradition of this kind exists in large parrots, in respect of fruiting tree distribution (which is patchy in both space and time) within given areas; there is no reason it should not occur in flamingos. At any rate, we know that the various, seemingly isolated breeding populations of flamingos are in touch with each other. This is not so hard to believe in the flamingos of the New World, since their ranges are relatively constrained (the only exception may be the "stranded" population of Caribbean Flamingos in the Galápagos); nor is it so difficult to credit in the western Mediterranean populations of the Greater Flamingo. However, the extreme scatter in some of the African and Asian Greater and Lesser Flamingo populations suggests their full isolation, although evidence indicates contact, or certainly travel between established sites, on at least an irregular basis. Ringing has shown that birds as far north-east as Kazakhstan occasionally visit the western Mediterranean, and that birds from Iran may travel south-east to the eastern Mediterranean and then follow the Rift Valley south into East Africa.

The largely resident Lesser and Greater Flamingos at Makgadikgadi Pan in Botswana appear to have created an "overflow" area at Etosha Pan in Namibia, almost 1,000 km (620 mi) to the east, where breeding is only extremely sporadic (five times in the 18 years from 1956 to 1973). Moreover, Makgadikgadi's Lesser Flamingos are thought to receive substantial immigrants from East Africa, as for example in late 1974 when all the lakes in Kenya and Tanzania showed a pronounced dip in numbers and the Botswana concentration soared to a million birds. The two other outlying populations of Lesser Flamingo, right across Africa in southern Mauritania and far up in north-east India in Kutch, also appear to make sporadic contact with birds from the core population in East Africa. However, it is still conceivable that undiscovered breeding colonies exist in intervening areas, perhaps helping to bridge the extraordinary distances involved. Flamingos fly mostly at night, and at 55 km/h (34 mph) they cannot expect to travel further than 600 km (370 mi) between dusk and dawn, which is already a tremendous feat. It may be that sometimes they simply keep going (airmen have reported flamingos flying at great heights, suggesting both eagle-avoidance and habitat-searching); or it may be that they put down in little-known water bodies where they can rest for the day without feeding. Between Makgadikgadi and Etosha, for example, sits the great Okavango Swamp, and this may be used as an occasional staging area.

One notable finding in Greater Flamingos is that young birds in the Camargue in southern France disperse in the direction of the prevailing wind – whether east or west is simply a matter of chance. However, whatever the direction of the wind in following years, the birds always return to the winter quarters that they reached at the end of their first summer. This tends to argue for the idea that the flamingo's map of the world is drawn by experience and not by ancestral instinct.

The brooded youngster frequently puts its head out to watch the world and beg to be fed
Photograph © Helio & Van Ingen, NHPA

SADLY

that map of the world is shrinking. The post-industrial emergence of *Homo sapiens* as the dominant species on the planet is forcing all wildlife, except for the weeds and commensals, into retreat. Animals with specialised habits, strongly adapted to stable environments, are among the most vulnerable to the changes man brings. Long-lived, slow-breeding creatures, adapted to compete amongst themselves for resources, are exposed and susceptible when major perturbations of their environments take place. They cannot cope with declines in habitat quality; they simply decline with them. And they are unable to recover rapidly from disastrous losses, since their intrinsic rate of increase is so small. All flamingos belong to this steadily retreating camp.

It is true that flamingos continue to achieve a degree of security by the very remoteness of their sites; compared to many other waterbirds, for which the wholesale conversion of wetlands to farmland and rice paddy has caused massive losses of numbers, the flamingos have fared, for the present, moderately well. But remoteness is a relative quantity in the twenty-first century, and none of their breeding grounds is as remote as it was a hundred or even fifty years ago, when those of the Lesser and Puna Flamingos were still waiting to be discovered. Worse, the danger with flamingos is their all-or-nothing use of a site. Most other waterbird species express habitat loss as a thinning of overall numbers. For flamingos habitat and location are virtually synonymous: to date, the rewards of their habitat specialisation have meant our planet has been graced by six wonderful species of bird; but the risks of such specialisation are now in the ascendant, and it may not be too long before we find ourselves in a long struggle to save every one of them.

The species at greatest risk are the two diatom specialists of South America, the Andean and Puna Flamingos. A four-country census in 1997 revealed that only around 34,000 of the former, the bulk of them in Chile, and 48,000 of the latter, the great majority in Bolivia, survive. These are trifling numbers by comparison with those of other species, and there is concern that human impacts on certain key nesting and feeding lakes — mining, water extraction, egg-harvesting, general disturbance — has had, and could yet have, dramatic repercussions on the birds. The situation may be scarcely different for the Lesser Flamingo. Despite being the world's most numerous species, in some regards it may be as precariously placed as the Andean birds. This is because, like them, it has so few core areas in which to breed. In the Rift Valley its chief haunts (arranged north to south, the first four in Kenya, the last three in Tanzania) are Lake Bogoria (formerly Hannington); Lake Nakuru (where it once bred); Lake Elmenteita (where it occasionally attempts to breed); Lake Magadi (where it bred once, in 1962); Lake Natron (where it breeds in huge numbers); the "remote, jewel-like" Embagai Crater in the Ngorongoro Plateau; and Lake Manyara. For years now this population has been reproductive at only a single site, Lake Natron in Tanzania. Natron fills with water for only a few weeks each year as rain drains off the highlands to the north, in Kenya; for the rest of the time it steadily dries out, exposing vast beds of sodium carbonate which form a brittle crust over miles and miles of soft mud. Even in this vastness, such is the natural variability in rainfall and salinity that the birds sometimes go for as many as seven years at a stretch without attempting to nest.

OVERLEAF: *The evil glistening heart of Lake Natron, which almost claimed the life of Leslie Brown*

The immediate difficulty for the conservationist is to know just how rigid the Lesser Flamingo is in its rejection of Bogoria, Nakuru, Magadi, Embagai and Manyara as nesting sites. The fact that it has attempted to breed at Elmenteita, but has never succeeded, is clearly worrying. Are conditions really so exacting that these places can provide for the birds in abundance and yet not grant them sufficient latitude to breed? Does this mean, in effect, that the species is exclusively dependent on Lake Natron for its survival in the Rift Valley, and indeed everywhere? Can we expect its smaller outlying populations — even those in India and West Africa — to persist in the long term if, in that common euphemism we always use of ourselves, "something happened" to the powerhouse colony at the heart of its range?

For indeed something *is* poised to happen to the great powerhouse of Lake Natron, which still has no statutory protection from the Tanzanian government.

Kenya now has plans to build a hydroelectric-cum-irrigation dam on the Ewaso Ngiro river (the lake's chief feeder) after diverting other rivers to improve its flow. The result would be an increase in the volume of fresh water in Lake Natron as well as in the chemical fertilisers suspended in that water: both of these factors would alter dramatically the ecology of the lake. Furthermore, a soda extraction plant has for years been proposed there, building on the Magadi model 25 km (15 mi) to the north. Given the position and size of the lake, a pipeline and great quantities of water would be needed in order to pump the soda as slurry all the way to the coast, and the water would also, of course, come from the lake, with catastrophic consequences (these irrespective of the disturbance such a plant might create). Leslie Brown thought the Natron colonies "as safe from the interference of mortal man as any bird's breeding ground is ever likely to be". Sadly, he was wrong.

And then there is Lake Nakuru, another closed system which loses water only through evaporation. Nakuru was declared a national park in 1968 in recognition of its extraordinary ornithological value. Indeed, it was the first national park in tropical Africa to be created solely on account of its bird life. Not infrequently over a million flamingos concentrate on its $42km^2$ ($16mi.^2$) surface, furnishing one of the undisputed wildlife spectacles of the planet. But the national park status is no prophylactic against the effects of pollution. The town of Nakuru, whose population grew tenfold from 30,000 in 1960 to 300,000 in 1995, has industries (such as a battery factory and a tannery) which produce highly toxic materials, with no effective sewage treatment. Intensifying agriculture around the edges of the lake has produced a constant run-off of pesticides and chemical fertilisers, compounded by erosion of soil through unwise slope farming and the clearance of forest. There is now widespread dismay at the way man-made compounds and effluents are accumulating in the lake, and a descending sense of foreboding that the great wildlife spectacle there may come to an end, forever. The birds have largely gone and, until the lake is restored to their peculiar standards (if this is still feasible), they may never return.

We know from Leslie Brown's research that Lake Bogoria and the Embagai Crater are not well suited to breeding, however good they are as feeding areas. Moreover, Lake Bogoria experienced a mass death involving some 25,000 Lesser Flamingos in late 1993. This was subsequently attributed to the bacterium *Pseudomonas aeruginosa*, a natural phenomenon, and judged to be no great cause for alarm; but within months of the beginning of the new millennium large numbers of birds there were once more reported to be dying. While again the cause appeared to be natural, there is always a concern that small shifts in chemical compositions at such a lake, owing to the effects of man, may promote adverse conditions for the birds. Meanwhile, at Lake Manyara, although a portion of it is a national park, there is anecdotal evidence of a greatly reduced freshwater inflow, probably the result of new local irrigation systems, expanding human populations, continuing forest clearance and water extraction for tourist developments.

The fear must be that each of the major flamingo lakes in the Rift Valley provides an essential service to the species as a whole. Imagine a series of stepping stones in a river: if one is washed away, the value of all the others is reduced to nothing – you cannot get across. The precautionary principle requires us to consider that each of East Africa's seven major Lesser Flamingo lakes is essential in some way to the survival of the species. It is certainly true that all seven are needed to maintain the sheer numerical spectacle of the Lesser Flamingo. (This applies equally to the Greater Flamingo, whose population across the same seven lakes is in the order of 50,000 birds, breeding at Lakes Elmenteita and Natron.)

On this basis, therefore, it is vitally important to secure Lakes Natron and Nakuru from any further development, and to restore Nakuru to its former status. And the other main lakes – Elmenteita, Magadi, Embagai and Manyara – will also require careful management and conservation. These systems are inherently and irreversibly fragile – they hold one of the natural wonders of the world in their metaphorical hands. There is much yet to do if the pinkness at the heart of Africa is to be saved forever.

OVERLEAF:
The patterns of soda and water in Lake Bogoria are reflected by the flamingos

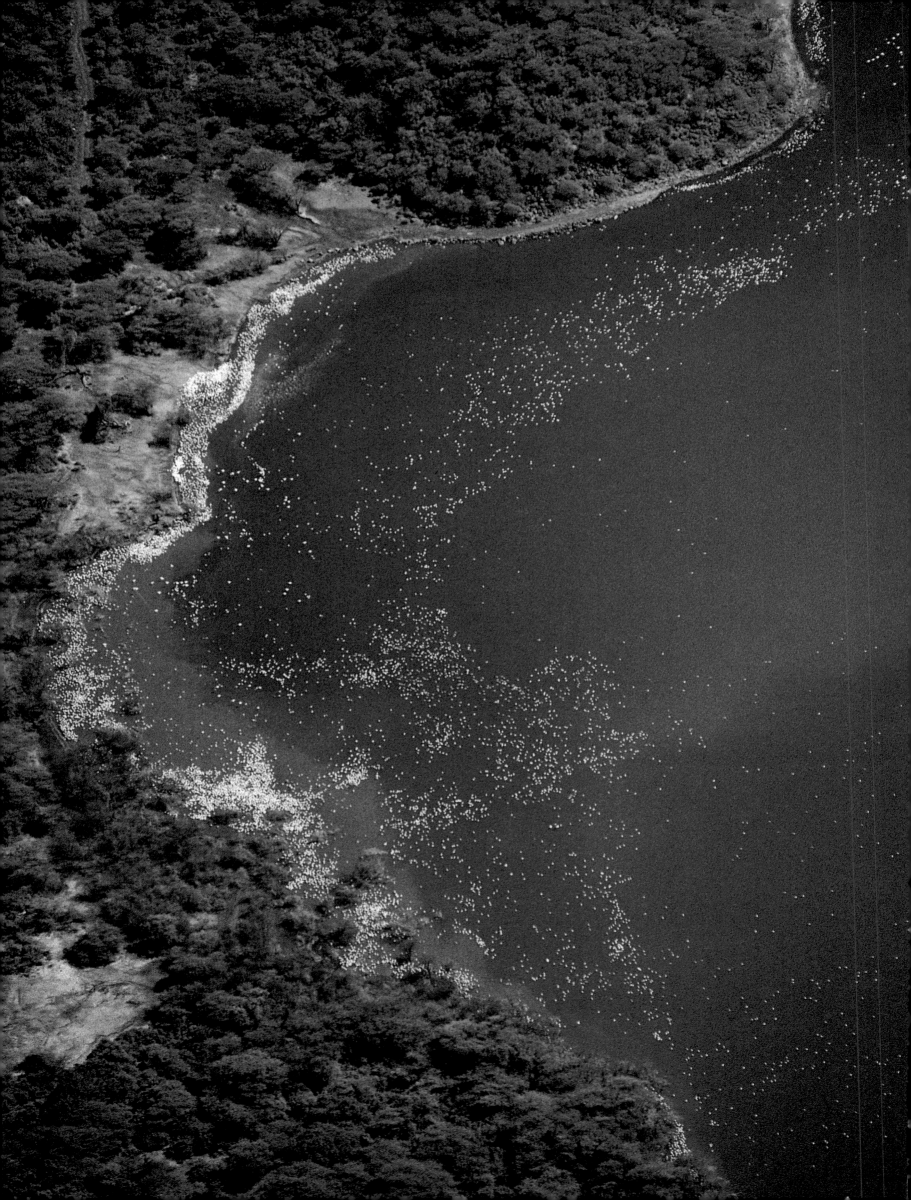

TOGETHERNESS IN FLAMINGOS

creates unforgettable beds of pink in the Rift Valley. Although the two species usually make their own separate flocks, they sometimes find themselves intermingling. Solitary birds are not solitary for long, and such exclusion is often a sign of illness. Lesser Flamingos in particular pack themselves tight, especially when parading in display, their legs forming a "red winkling forest". They also bunch together when they take flight and when they feed, creating gorgeous patterns as they concentrate on the richest areas.

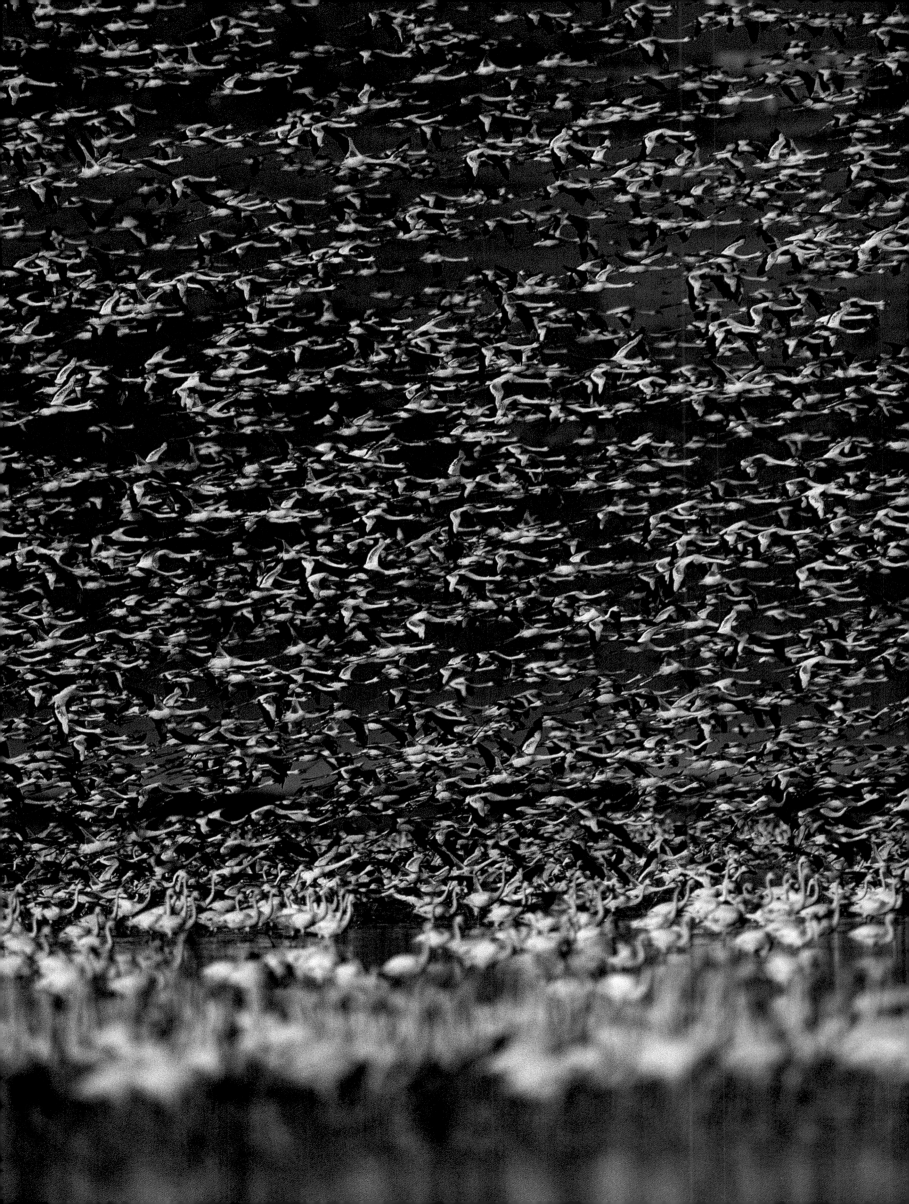

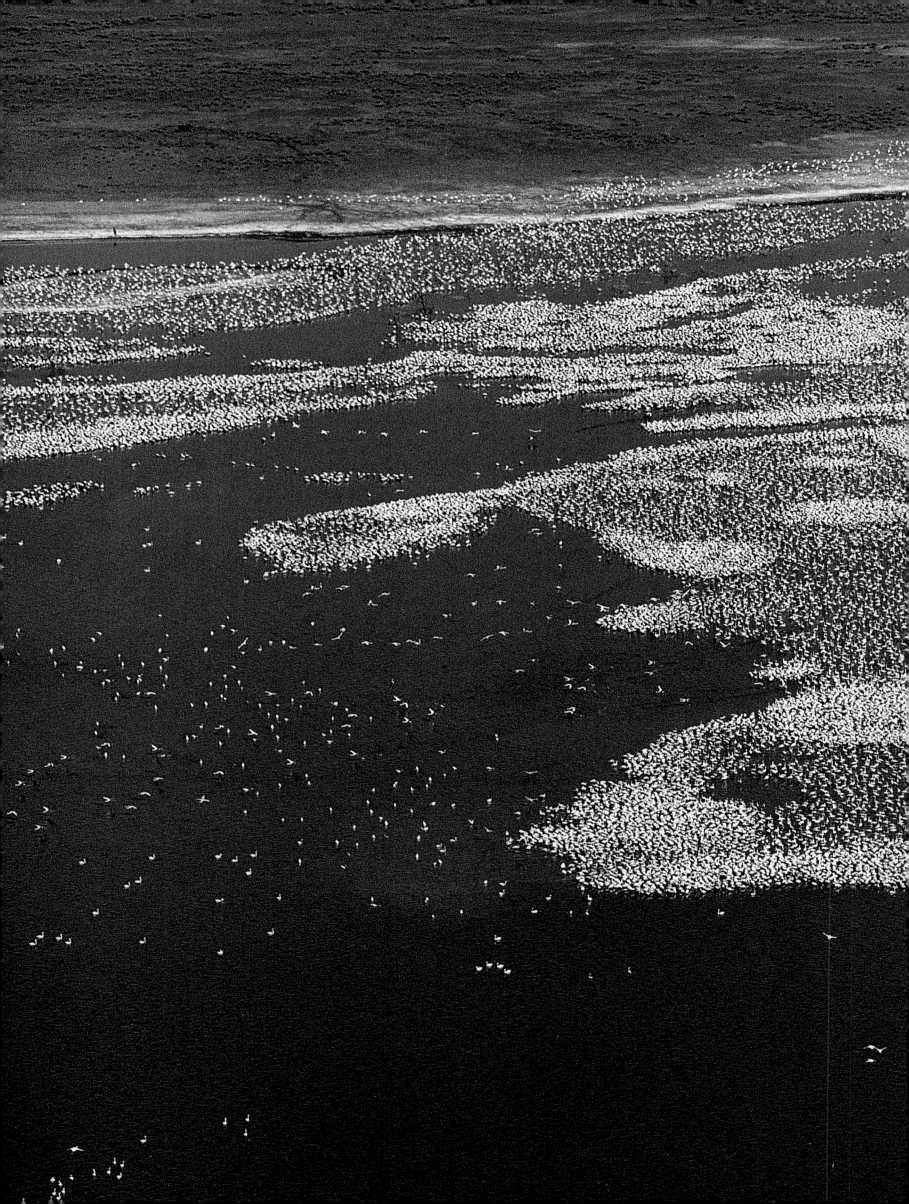

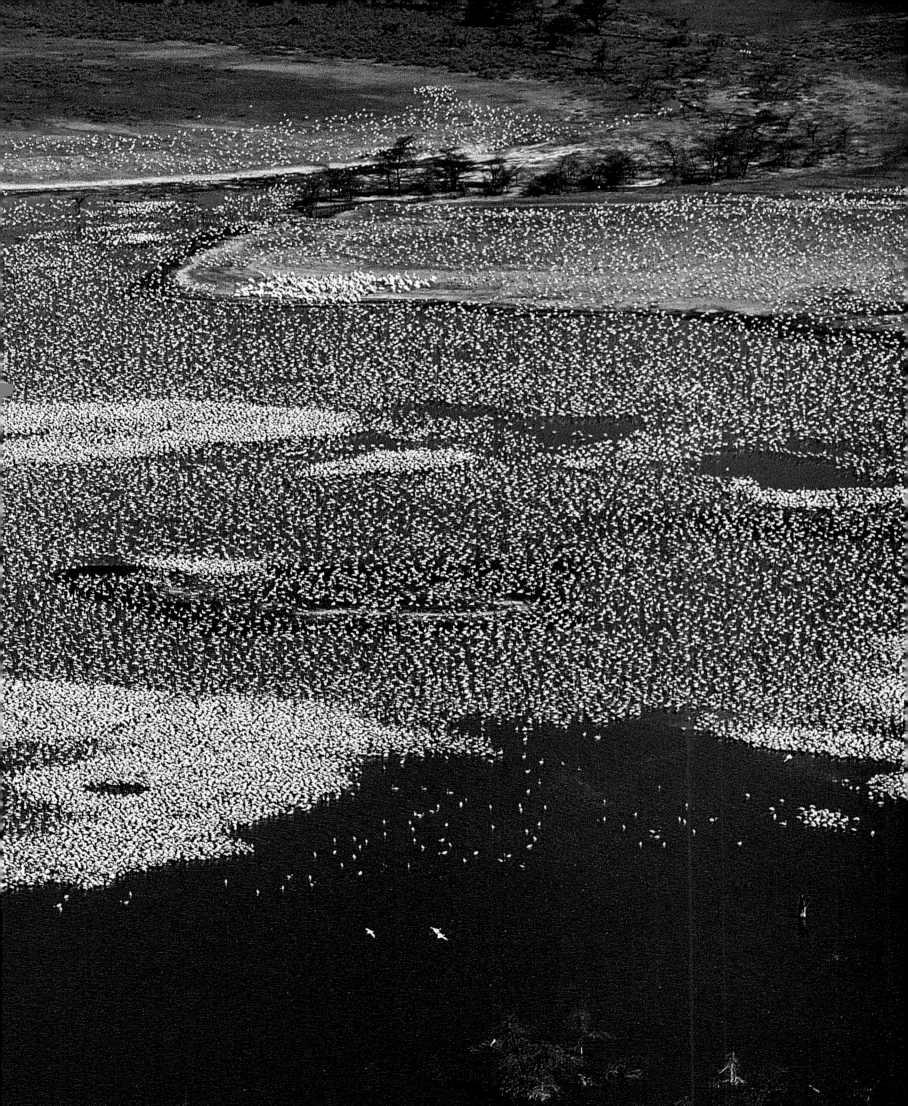

THE PINKNESS OF THE FLAMINGOS

comes from compounds in the microscopic foods they eat, but it gets distributed at different intensities in different parts of the birds. The shading varies with species and season. Lesser Flamingos are overall much pinker than the Greaters, but also have brilliant crimson bases to the underwing, and mauve-tinged crimson upperwing-coverts, creating a distinctive pattern as they fly.

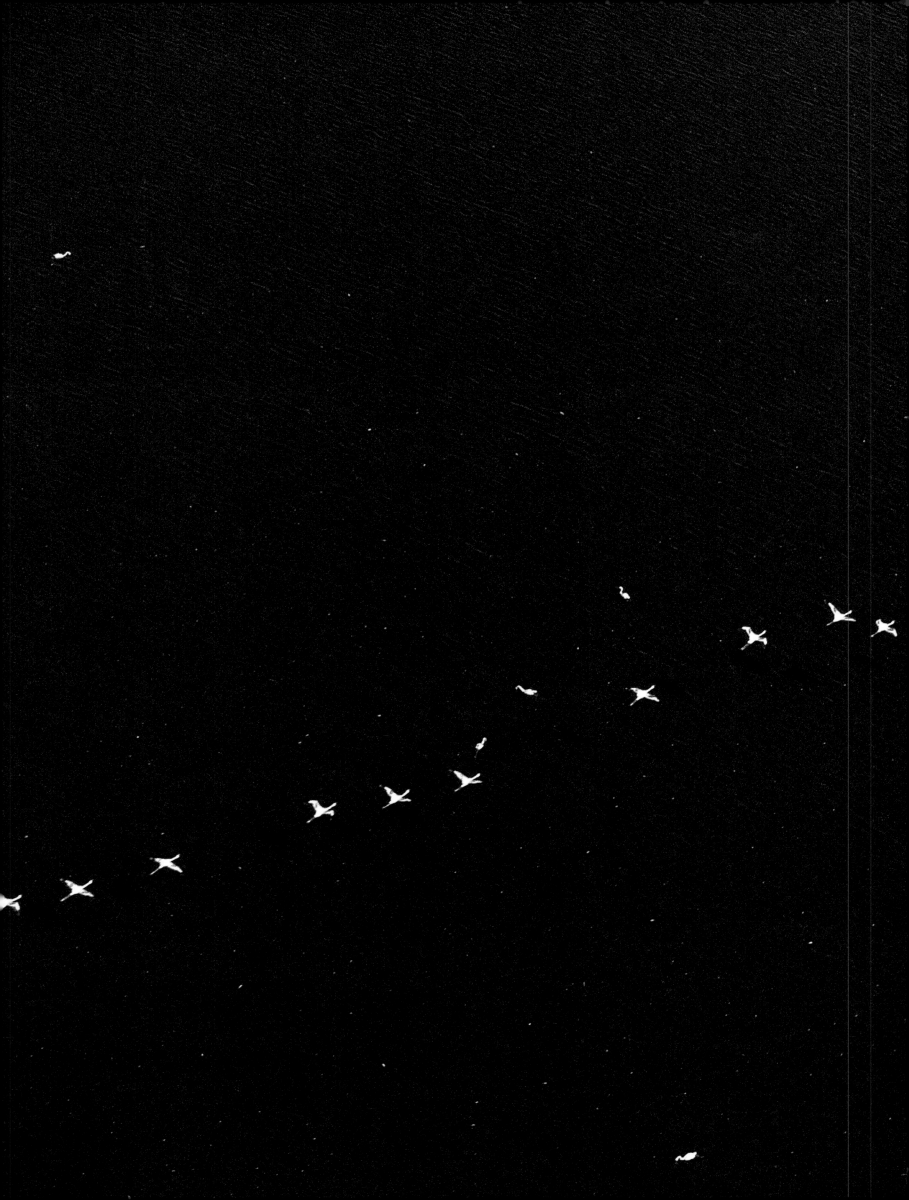

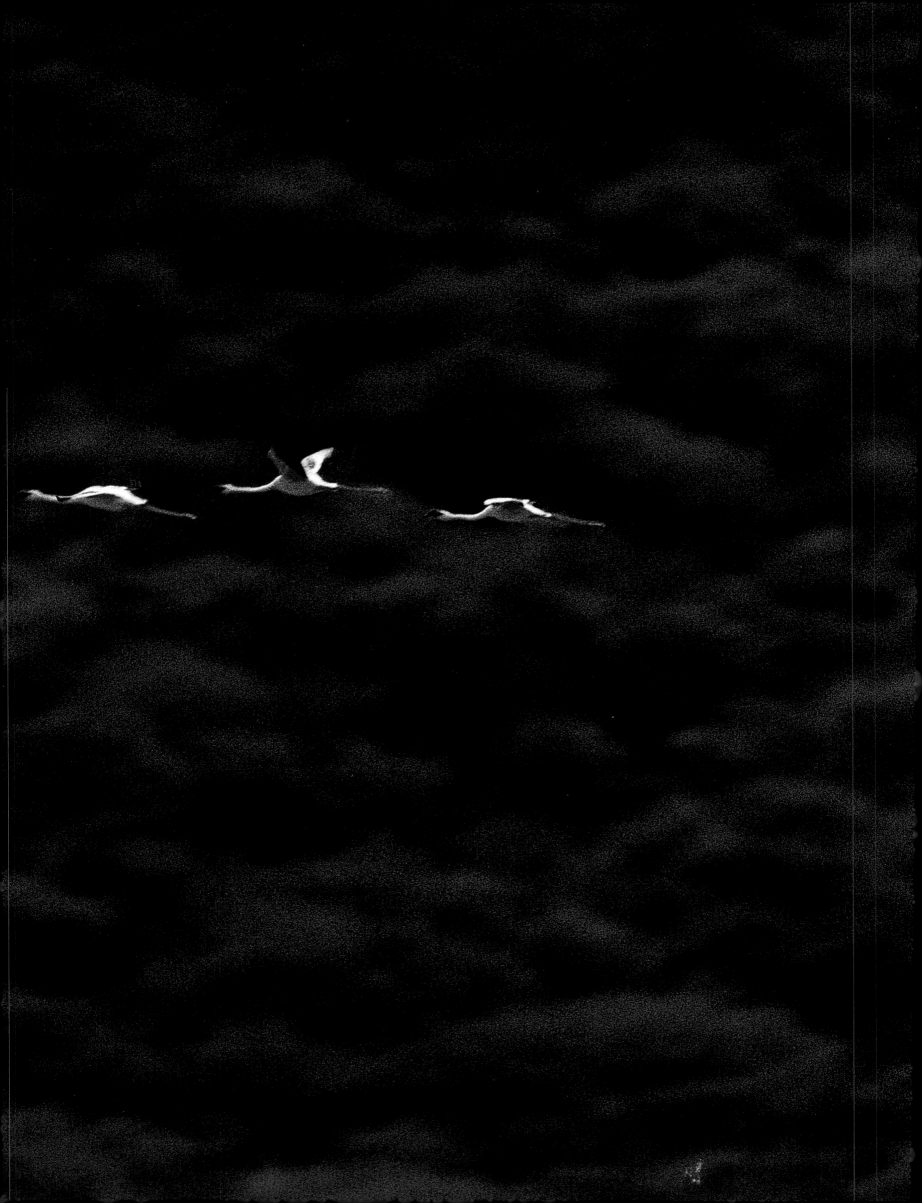

ASSEMBLING FOR A FEEDING SESSION

at Lake Bogoria, a flock of Lesser Flamingos shows the striking
contrast between their pink bodies and red legs. They shift places,
looking for the best concentrations of food, before settling on a good
area. Favoured areas are often littered with feathers, which come out
when birds pause to preen or as they flap up to get closer to the flock.

A SHORELINE STREWN WITH FEATHERS

reveals a major roosting area for Lesser Flamingos, where some birds linger to drink. Two birds at Lake Bogoria | *previous pages* | use their bills to squabble mildly while the others slake their thirst. Elsewhere the water is usually too acrid to drink, and it gets into the birds' feathers (especially when they upend in deeper water) so they have to spend much time preening.

| *Opposite* | The corrosive shores of Lake Natron are a combination of crystalline soda and volcanic rubble.

LAKE NATRON IS THE MOST HOSTILE

of all the Rift Valley flamingo lakes | *following pages* |. Sometimes it
looks like the surface of another planet, an acrid chemical mix
where no-one would expect to find life. At other times it looks like
a snowfield, the birds feeding on ice-crystals.

| *Opposite* | One of the soda beaches at Lake Bogoria where the
flamingos regularly come to feed, its concentration of blue-green
algae being perenially high

THE REMARKABLE BILL OF THE LESSER FLAMINGO.

Like a baleen whale in shape and structure, and evolved for the same purpose, the flamingo's grotesque bill is heavily arched to maximise the quantity of food it can hoover up using the hair-like lamellae along and inside the mandibles to trap great quantities of microscopic algae.

| *Overleaf* | Lake Elmenteita, one of the less hostile alkaline lakes.

THE TRANQUILITY OF THE FLAMINGO LAKES IS DECEPTIVE.

Apart from the astringency of the water, Lake Bogoria has geothermal springs and geysers around its shores, producing piping hot water. The birds prefer this rather fresher water for drinking, but its heat sometimes makes them dance uncomfortably.

| *Following pages* | Then there are the Marabous, the Undertaker Birds. Mostly they appear to be content to scavenge, since in huge flocks of flamingos one or two birds are always dying. Sometimes, however, the storks lose patience and go for a living bird. A Marabou can kill a flamingo just by flying into a flock and grabbing its delicate neck as it takes wing. But usually it will spot a straggler, a sick bird, one moving slower than the others. The spectacle is unpleasant, but the end is swift.

PREDATION MAY BE ONE OF THE KEY FACTORS

in flamingos moving from lake to lake, or from one part of a lake to another. The panic after a Marabou attack is followed by a more measured dispersal to safer places. The flamingos are always assessing and balancing several environmental factors – how much food, how many feeders, how many predators – and shifting their areas accordingly.

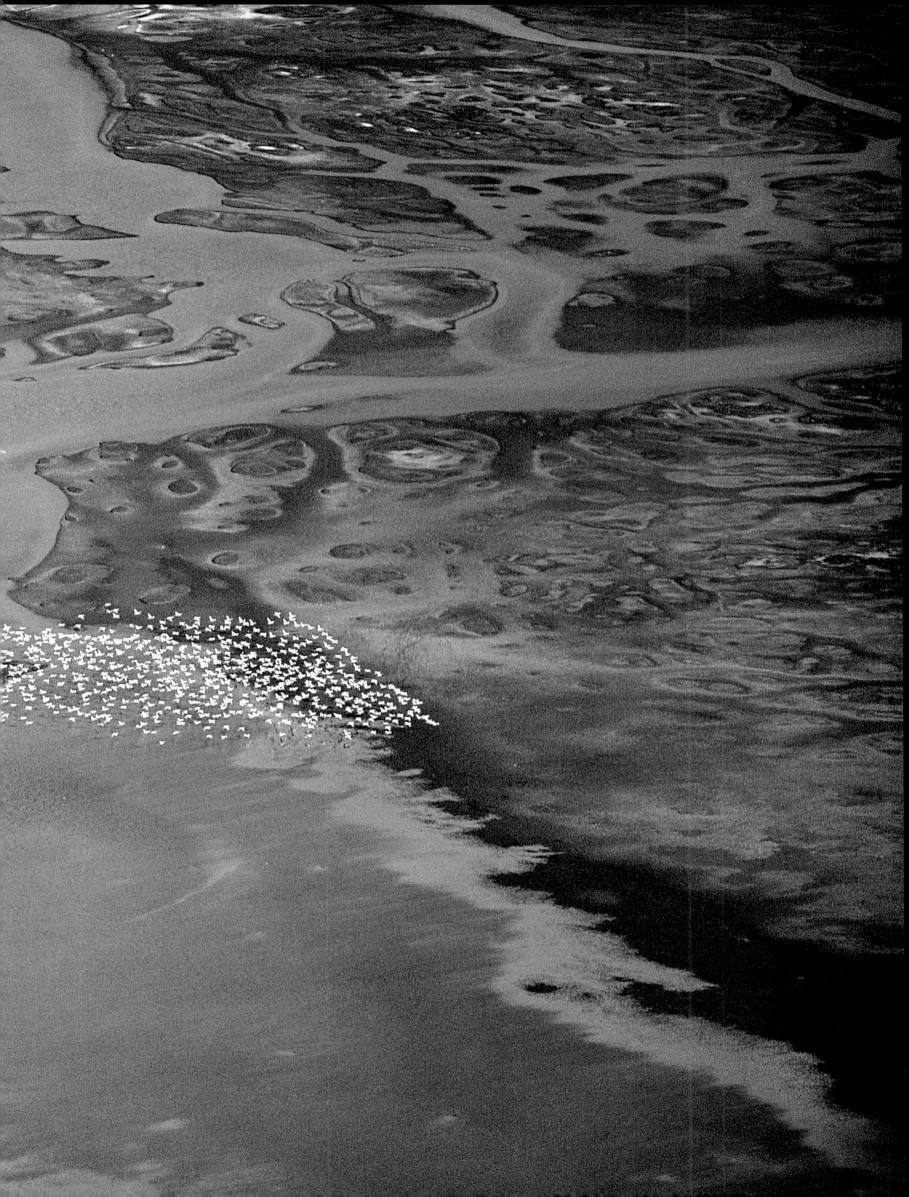

THE LARGER GREATER FLAMINGO

takes much bigger prey than the Lesser. Preening the feathers prepares Lesser Flamingos for another bout of feeding, which may be in the shallows or it may be in deeper water. In the shalllows the birds usually let their bills float at the surface as the heads sweep back and forth. In deeper water they sometimes upend like ducks to reach the bottom. In deeper still they readily swim, looking like a flock of gangly geese, raking their bills through the surface of the lake.

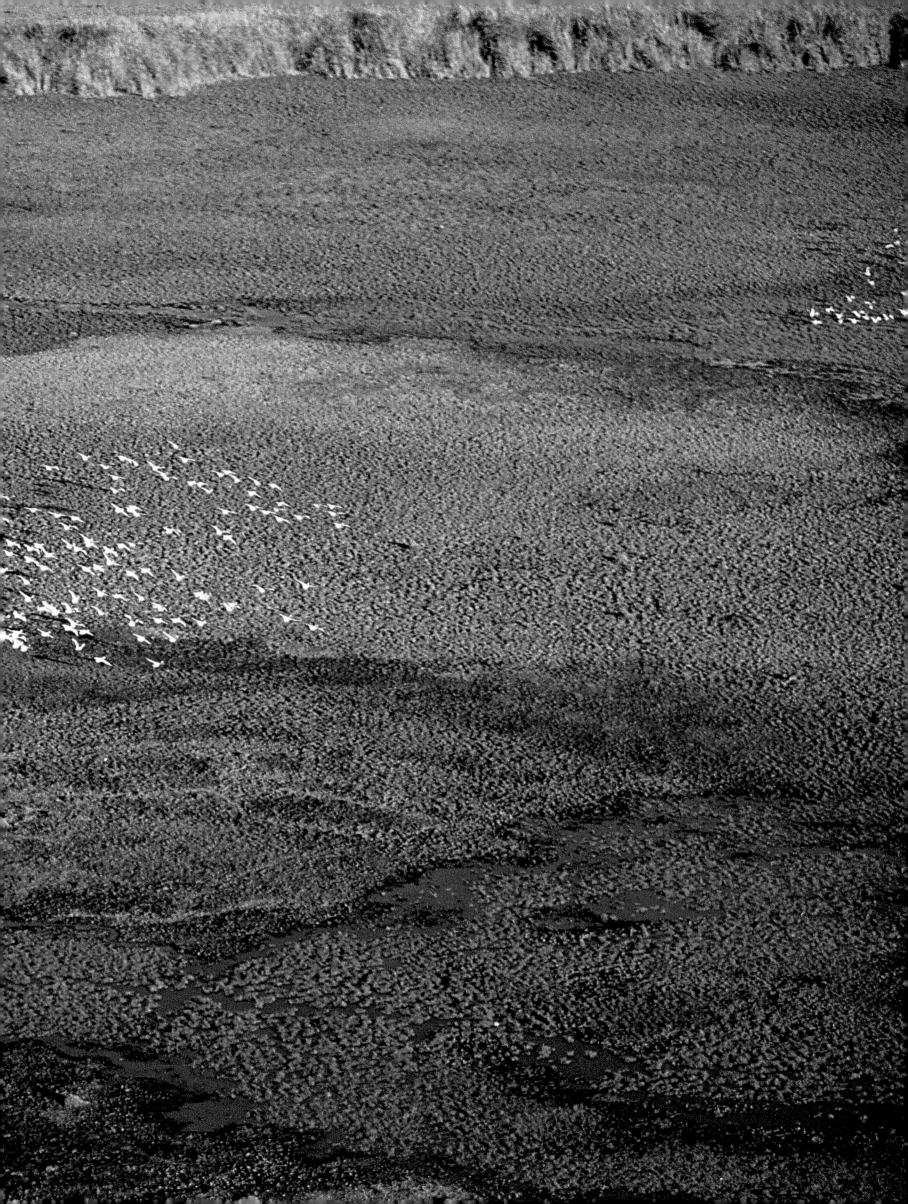

LAKE NATRON IS NOT ALWAYS FORBIDDING.

| *Opposite and preceding pages* | When it fills with seasonal fresh water from the Kenyan highlands, there are flushes of green plant life and stretches of blue water that briefly make it almost inviting. | *Overleaf* | Lake Elmenteita, one of the more easily accessible soda lakes to humans.

BIRDS THAT LIVE IN HUGE GROUPS

are often prone to outbreaks of disease. At the start of 2000, Lake Bogoria's Lesser Flamingo population suddenly began to show signs of an epidemic. Sick birds would become detached from the flock, stagger pathetically for an hour or two, losing all coordination, then fall and drown in the shallows or collapse on the shore. Some years ago a similar outbreak was traced to a naturally occurring bacterium, but there are always worries that such events are rooted in some unsuspected environmental damage wrought by man.

DIE-OFF

amongst the flamingos is good news for the scavengers – chiefly the Marabou, but even a young Sacred Ibis will feed up on a fresh corpse.

RAINS BRING MUCH-NEEDED FRESH WATER

to the land-locked lakes of the Rift Valley, and with it the promise of new feeding and drinking areas for the flamingos. But when the rain is falling, as here at Lake Bogoria, the feeding conditions are too disturbed, so the birds go into sleep mode, necks retracted and everyone huddled together... until a passing dog decides to try for an exotic lunch.

AS NIGHT COMES ON AT LAKE BOGORIA,

the flamingos may carry on feeding, especially if the day's routine
has been interrupted by rain or dogs. Egrets gather to roost in trees
out of the reach of dogs. Alongside them, a few Marabou perch as
well – the sinister presence of the Undertaker Bird will always haunt
the flamingos, however distantly they may go to nest, however large
the flocks they make.

LIVING AT THE VERY EDGE OF ENDURANCE,

hemmed in by their own defencelessness on the one hand and by the
brutal severity of their environment on the other, the flamingos step
into the future with their own peculiar grace and dignity.

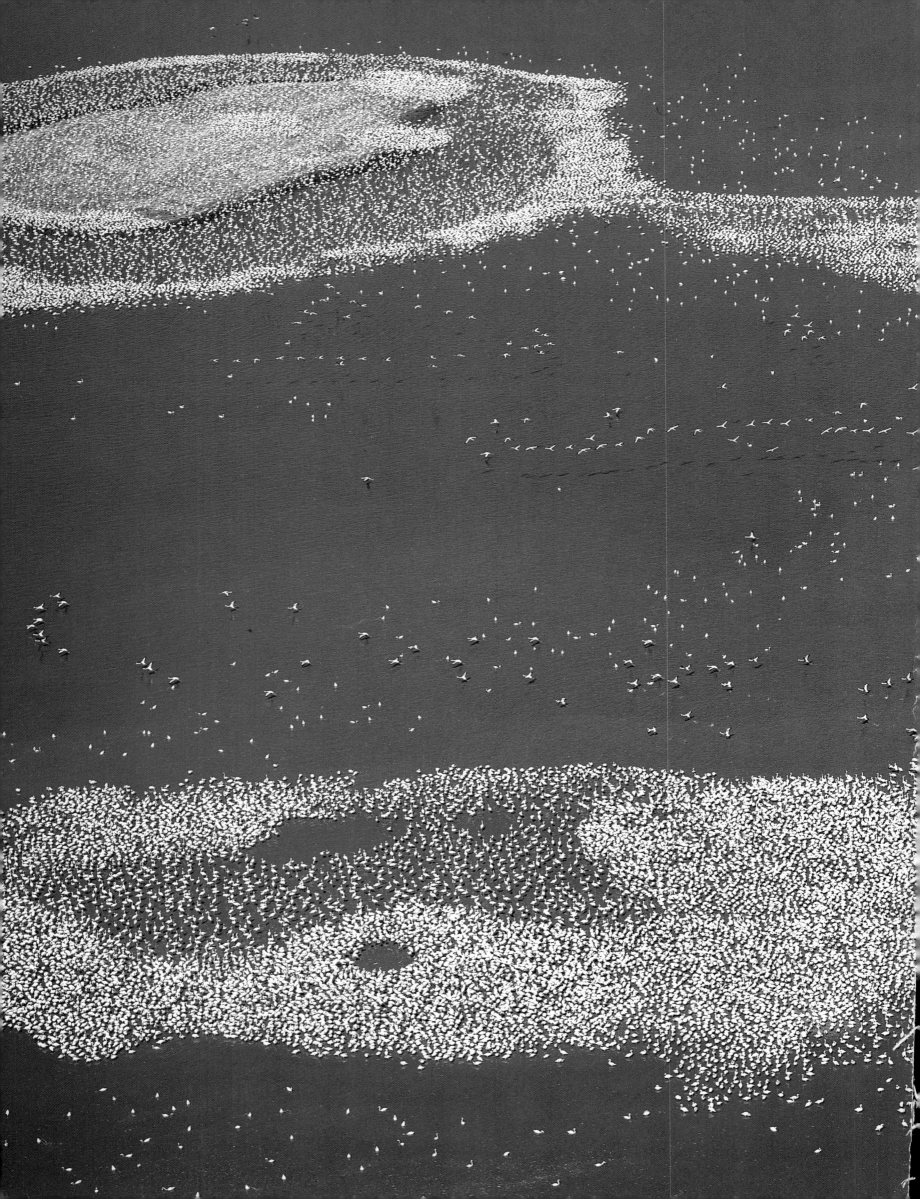